Creative Strategies
for Teaching
World Geography

HOLT, RINEHART AND WINSTON

Harcourt Brace & Company

Austin • New York • Orlando • Atlanta • San Francisco • Boston • Dallas • Toronto • London

The Authors

Nancy Lehmann-Carssow is a geography teacher at Lanier High School, Austin, Texas. Mrs. Lehmann-Carssow received her B.S. and M.A. from the University of Texas in geography and anthropology. She has also studied at the University of Nairobi, Kenya Science Teacher's College, Hebrew University, and George Washington University. She has written curriculum guides, made presentations at social studies conventions on the national, state, and local levels, and served on local and state textbook committees. Mrs. Lehmann-Carssow received a Fulbright Scholarship to Israel in 1983, attended the first National Geographic Institute in Washington D.C., received the Certificate of Meritorious Teaching Achievement from the National Council for Geographic Education, and has twice been a finalist for Teacher of the Year in Austin. She has incorporated her extensive travels in Africa, Asia, South America, Europe, and Australia into her teaching. Mrs. Lehmann-Carssow is a founding member of the Texas Alliance for Geographic Education.

Mary Catherine Martin received her B.A. and M.Ed. from the University of Texas at Austin. She has worked as a Process Evaluator with the Austin Independent School District, Office of Research and Evaluation; as an elementary and secondary social studies teacher at Saint Louis Catholic School, Austin, Texas; and as a geography teacher at Stephen F. Austin High School, Austin, Texas. Ms. Martin has received several teaching awards, including the Creative Teaching Award in 1984 and 1985, the Parent Teacher Student Association Teaching Excellence Award in 1993, and Teacher of the Year at Austin High School in 1990. Professional activities have included writing geography curriculum for the Austin Independent School District, and presenting workshops, papers, and teaching techniques at national, state, and local professional meetings. Her educational travels have included most of the United States, Asia, Africa, Australia, Europe, and New Zealand. Ms. Martin is currently working as an educational consultant and with the Earth Foundation of Houston, Texas, an organization dedicated to the preservation of the earth's rain forest environment.

Printed in the United States of America

ISBN 0-03-054478-5

12 13 14 095 07 06 05

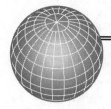

To the Teacher

Creative Strategies for Teaching World Geography provides you with opportunities to teach important geographical concepts using activities that will generate enthusiasm and invite independent thinking in your classroom. The extended strategies use games, simulations, reader's theater, and case studies to engage students in their study of world regional geography. Included in the lessons are detailed instructions to the teacher, reproducible resource materials and handouts for students, and supporting teaching transparencies.

The lessons cover a wide range of subjects. Students might design and create their own African *kanga*—a garment worn in many parts of Africa, devise a plan for saving the world's rain forests, play a Bingo game based on the physical and human geography of India, plan a "dream vacation" to a foreign country, test their own preconceived and perhaps erroneous ideas about other lands and peoples, and learn about contributions from other cultures to their own culture.

The methods used in *Creative Strategies for Teaching World Geography* provide tremendous flexibility in the classroom. The content can be modified to use the same lesson again and again with other units. Lesson 5, for example, "Using the Mural Method to Study Culture: A Case Study of the Mbuti" is appropriate for a unit on aspects of culture, culture traits, and cultural diffusion. However, this lesson can be modified for other units as well. Although it focuses on the cultural traits of a hunting and gathering society, the mural method and "ABCs of Culture" can easily be applied to other types of culture groups and societies.

Contents

Understanding Absolute Location: Spy Tracking

Creative Strategies

BACKGROUND

Earth can be divided into a northern and southern hemisphere by a great circle of latitude—the equator (0 degrees latitude). All lines of latitude run parallel to the equator and are called parallels. Latitude is determined by applying the principle that there are 360 degrees in a circle (or sphere). Divisions of 360 degrees are stated as angles. The degree of the angle determines the degree of latitude. Parallels of latitude run east and west but measure distance north and south of the equator. The highest reading of latitude possible is 90 degrees north or south.

The same principles of geometry apply to longitude. The degree of the angle determines the degree of longitude. Every line of longitude is one-half of a great circle and is called a meridian. The highest reading of longitude is 180 degrees.

PROCEDURE

Students will work with a partner to "solve" the mystery given in the handout. Then have each pair write its own story using the concepts of latitude and longitude. These stories may be turned in for a grade or evaluation, read aloud to the rest of the class, or exchanged among students for additional practice on using latitude and longitude to determine absolute location.

Answers to "Understanding Absolute Location: Spy Tracking" handout:

1. a. Middle of the Indian Ocean
   b. Boat; Pacific Ocean

2. Austin, Texas; Colorado (in Texas)

3. Sahara; heat exhaustion

4. (student choice); (student choice); Hawaii

RECOMMENDED TIME

• One class period

OBJECTIVES

• Use latitude and longitude to determine absolute location

• Develop map skills

MATERIALS

• Handout: "Understanding Absolute Location: Spy Tracking" for each student

• World atlas or textbook atlas

UNDERSTANDING ABSOLUTE LOCATION: SPY TRACKING

1. You are a member of an international spy ring which has decided that you are a secret agent who knows too much. The word is out that you must meet with a serious "accident." You begin to be suspicious when:

   a. Your helicopter pilot suddenly yells at you to bail out over 20 degrees south latitude and 70 degrees east longitude. Where are you?

   b. A passing vehicle picks you up and takes you to 40 degrees north latitude and 160 degrees east longitude. The crew hands you a huge rock and screams "JUMP!" What kind of vehicle picked you up and where did it take you? You are still wondering why they gave you a rock!

2. When you finally, against all odds, make it to a place just north of 30 degrees north latitude and just east of 98 degrees west longitude, you are exhausted and need rest. Where are you now? How could you have picked such a ridiculous place to stop? As a highly paid secret agent, you should have known about the nest of spies headquartered just north of the _____ River.

3. You still have not wised up and foolishly contact a fellow secret agent. She tells you that you can get plenty of rest if you go to 23½ degrees north latitude and 15 degrees east longitude. She even gives you plenty of warm clothes to make you more comfortable while you are there. When you arrive at 23½ degrees north latitude and 15 degrees east longitude you put on your fur-lined boots and parka and are suffering greatly by the time you realize your mistake. Where are you? What are you suffering from? _____ _____

4. By now you are aware that something strange is going on. You decide to invite your fellow spies to join you at _____ degrees (north or south) latitude and _____ degrees (east or west) longitude. To insure secrecy, you must plan the location and the fate of your colleagues, who have tried so hard to do you in. Share this information only with the Chief of Latitude Intelligence (your teacher). If s/he approves of your choice, s/he will reward you with approval for a trip to _____, which is located between 15 degrees north latitude and 30 degrees north latitude, and between 150 degrees west longitude and 170 degrees west longitude.

5. Now you must create your own latitude and longitude story using at least five locations. Write a spy story, a love story, or whatever you like. Be creative!

Understanding Absolute and Relative Location: Where in the World?

Creative Strategies

BACKGROUND

Every place on Earth has a location. **Location** is defined in terms of absolute and relative location. Absolute location is a physical site—the exact spot on Earth where something is found. For example, Niamey, the capital of Niger, is located at 13° 31' north latitude and 2° 07' east longitude. Relative location is a situation—the position of a place in relation to other places. For example, Yosemite National Park is located north of Los Angeles, California, and east of San Francisco, California.

PROCEDURE

Before beginning the activity, have students review absolute and relative location by asking them to describe the location of their own city or school. Place students in groups of two to four people. One member of each group should act as secretary and record the required information. Each group will use an atlas to select a specific city outside of the United States. After determining the city's absolute location, students in each group will offer to the rest of the class relative location "clues." The first person or group to correctly identify the city wins a prize (optional).

RECOMMENDED TIME
• One class period

OBJECTIVE
• Distinguish between absolute and relative location

MATERIALS
• Handout : "Absolute and Relative Location: Where in the World?"
• World atlas or textbook atlas for each group
• Prize (optional, teacher's choice)

ABSOLUTE AND RELATIVE LOCATION: WHERE IN THE WORLD?

1. Using an atlas, select a city outside of the United States and write down its absolute location. Then, describe its relative location.

2. Challenge the rest of the class to identify your group's selected city by giving at least three relative location clues. For example, if your city is Nairobi, Kenya, the clue might be: "I am a city located south of the equator. I am near the Indian Ocean. I am on the east coast of Africa."

3. The first person to raise his or her hand and correctly identify the city will receive a small reward.

4. Be prepared to point out your group's city on a world map or globe.

Themes of Geography: Place, Human-environment Interaction, and Movement

Creative Strategies

BACKGROUND

Every place on Earth has a location. **Location** is defined in terms of absolute and relative location. Absolute location is a physical site—the exact spot on Earth where something is found. Relative location is a situation—the position of a place in relation to other places.

Every **place** on Earth has special characteristics that make it different from every other place. Every place can be described in terms of its physical characteristics, including weather, land features, plants, and animals. Every place can be described in terms of its human features. These features include a place's peoples, their cultures, and their ideas.

People are constantly interacting with their surroundings. This geographic theme is called **human-environment interaction.** People adapt to their environment.

People, goods, and ideas move continuously. The **movement** of people, goods, and ideas is called spatial interaction. As the amount of movement and kinds of transportation change, so do other geographic features. For example, the movement of tourists into Yosemite National Park has created a need for a shuttlebus service.

A **region** is an area defined by common characteristics. Regions can be defined by more than more characteristic.

PROCEDURE

Students should review the Themes of Geography. Then organize students into groups of three to four. Each group will create a collage illustrating the concepts of place, human-environment interaction, and movement. Students should refer to their handout for help with identifying items which should be included in each category. Allow time for each group to display and discuss its finished collage. The grading key provided should be used as a checklist for students. It may also be used by the teacher to assign grades easily while students are giving an oral presentation of the elements in their collage.

RECOMMENDED TIME

- One to two class periods

OBJECTIVES

- Distinguish between concept of place as a physical environment and relationships within place as human interaction within the environment
- Investigate types of human land use
- Understand that movement refers to people, goods, and ideas

MATERIALS

- Handout: "Themes of Geography: Place, Human-environment Interaction, and Movement Collage"
- Old magazines, scissors, glue, and poster board or large sheets of paper

THEMES OF GEOGRAPHY: PLACE, HUMAN-ENVIRONMENT INTERACTION, AND MOVEMENT COLLAGE

INSTRUCTIONS:

1. Your group will create a collage illustrating the concepts of place, human-environment interaction, and movement.

2. Remember that PLACE deals with the *physical* and *human* features of an environment and HUMAN-ENVIRONMENT INTERACTION represents the *interaction* of people and their environment. Physical features are always present in a particular environment. Your collage must show how people use these features. For example, if a place characteristic of a particular environment is mountains, they might be used both for economic activities (lumbering) and as a source of recreation (skiing). A picture showing people skiing would illustrate place (the physical feature) and human-environment interaction (how people have modified their environment by clearing trees to allow for the ski slopes). Remember that MOVEMENT deals with the movement of goods, people, and ideas (ski lift, communication systems, transportation systems, trade, etc.).

3. Refer to the following list for help in selecting appropriate examples.

PLACE
Physical Characteristics:
- climate
- landforms
- vegetation (flora)
- animal life (fauna)
- soils
- bodies of water (oceans, seas, lakes, etc.)

Human Characteristics:
- population
- language
- religion
- forms of economic, social, and political organization

HUMAN-ENVIRONMENT INTERACTION
- land use: farming, recreation, transportation, etc.
- settlement patterns: villages, cities
- water use: dams, reservoirs, etc.

MOVEMENT
- transportation
- communications

4. Your collage should be approximately two feet by two feet and should be covered with examples. Provide a label for each picture.

TO EARN A GRADE OF "A," YOU MUST INCLUDE SOME LABELS EXPLAINING THE PICTURES YOU HAVE SELECTED.

GRADING KEY:

Concept of place shown clearly (20 points) _____

Concept of human-environment interaction shown clearly (20 points) _____

Concept of movement shown clearly (20 points) _____

Attractive and neat appearance (15 points) _____

Size is correct (15 points) _____

Labels of explanation provided (10 points) _____

The "ABCs of Culture": A Framework for Understanding Culture

Creative Strategies

BACKGROUND

The "ABCs of Culture" gives students a standardized framework from which to study different cultures. When students realize that all people share similar characteristics, they can expand their knowledge by investigating *why* various groups have certain traits or traditions and appreciate the many differing ways of life of other societies.

Researching information on these topics will reveal various ways people adapt to their environment and their impact on the environment. By studying others' interaction with the environment, students become more aware of their own actions. This strategy may be applied to any age group and any learning level. Groups of students may be given different cultures to study following the ABCs, or if materials are limited, groups may be given one of the ABCs, and combine their research to make a complete report on a single culture group. Since the ABCs use mnemonics, they are easy for students to remember.

The following books are recommended for background information on various cultural traditions.

Axtell, Roger E., ed. *Do's and Taboos Around the World*. New York: John Wiley & Sons, 1985.

Axtell, Roger E. *Gestures*. New York: John Wiley & Sons, 1991.

Panati, Charles. *Browser's Book of Beginnings*. Boston: Houghton Mifflin Co., 1984.

Panati, Charles. *Extraordinary Origins of Everyday Things*. New York: Harper & Row, 1987.

Panati, Charles. *Panati's Parade of Fads, Follies, and Manias*. New York: Harper Perennial, 1991.

PROCEDURE

Review with students the definition of *culture* as the *learned* ways of living of a group of people. Emphasize that we are not born knowing a certain language, food, etc. Ask students how we have contact with other cultures (war or conquest, trade, travel or exploration, immigration and emigration, mass media or communications, education). Display the overhead transparency "Basic

RECOMMENDED TIME
- One to three class periods

OBJECTIVES
- Recognize shared characteristics of all societies
- Explore a framework for studying different cultures
- Avoid ethnocentrism in studying other cultures

MATERIALS
- Various library books and magazines (*National Geographic* magazines are especially useful.)
- Transparency 1: "Basic Vocabulary Words and Elements of the ABCs of Culture, The ABCs of Culture"
- Handout: "Basic Vocabulary Words and Elements of the ABCs of Culture, The ABCs of Culture"

Vocabulary Words and Elements of the ABCs of Culture." Allow time for class discussion before organizing students into groups of four or five. Ask each group to select a culture group to study (or assign a culture group, if necessary). Have students in each group research and report on the elements of the ABCs of Culture as they apply to their assigned culture group. As an alternative, assign the class one culture group and have each group research *one* of the ABCs of Culture as it applies to the assigned culture group. Groups should then combine their research for a class report.

BASIC VOCABULARY WORDS AND ELEMENTS OF THE ABCs OF CULTURE

cultural geography/anthropology: study of *living* cultures

archaeology: study of *past* cultures

gregarious: likes to be with other people (we naturally want to be in groups that are similar to us)

cultural diffusion: borrowing from other cultures—food, clothing styles, etc.; spread of culture to another area

acculturation: process by which a person from one culture adopts traits of another culture

prejudice: unreasonable attitude or bias against a group or culture based on supposed characteristics

bias: personal, distorted judgment that influences objective perception; one-sided

stereotype: over-simplified, commonly held opinion of a person or group; often a composite of traits; generalizations about an entire group

ethnocentric: (ethno=cultural group; centric=at the center) believing that one's own culture is the best or better than others; negative if extreme; positive if establishes self-pride

xenophobia: (xeno=foreign; phobia=fear) a fear of foreigners or things foreign

"THE ABCs OF CULTURE"

Appearance: clothing (special occasions, colors, how it is worn, hats, uniforms); jewelry (special meaning—wedding ring, lapel pins); type of material (bought, handmade, imported); hair style (females in Peru: two pigtails=married; many pigtails=single); physical features (tall, short); makeup; tattoos; etc.

Belief System: religion, superstitions (all cultures have them: Last Supper—13 people there and last was Judas, salt spilled in front of him; step on a crack; lights on cars in funeral procession; etc.)

Communication: language; tone; signs; body language (82% of teacher messages are non-verbal); titles (presidents *vs* king *vs* chief); greetings (hand shakes); common words with different definitions: "Do you **mind** waiting for me?"; last names from jobs (Miller, Smith), physical features (Rivers, Hill); *Mc, von,* and *O'* all mean "son of," as in McDonald, von Huesen, O'Neill, and also Johnson, Jackson, etc.

Dates: history; ancestry; heritage; establish concepts of time—how is it important to society?; holidays; etc.

Entertainment: art; music; crafts; dance; sports; songs; storytelling; hobbies; etc.

Food: types; spices; special occasions; preparation; taboos; how people eat; number of meals a day and times eaten; fasting; etc.

Government: laws; values; titles; social roles and order (Do only women raise children? Are certain jobs reserved for men?); how people act toward each other (consider different age groups); social groups/clubs, etc.

Housing: style; materials; use of rooms; shape; size; color; arrangement of furniture; etc.

Information: informal (education from relatives and peers); formal (school, life experience)

Jobs: technology (scientific knowledge and tools); economy; ways of making a living; style/type of currency; transportation; communication; etc.

Kind of Environment: location; climate; physical features; vegetation (This information explains relationships to the environment, such as why the Inuit of the northern Arctic region eat raw meat and fish—there is no wood to burn for cooking; this also explains why there are many words in their language describing snow and ice.)

Leftovers: leftover information that doesn't fit into one of the above categories (population, diseases, etc.)

Remember that many items will fit into more than one category. Practice classifying items according to the ABCs of Culture. Determine the appropriate categories for these items: magnifying glass (J), birthday party (D), money (J).

Using the Mural Method to Study Culture: A Case Study of the Mbuti

Creative Strategies

BACKGROUND

This lesson uses a mnemonic (key words/s) and a picture to explore the customs of a culture group. The mnemonic enables students to "unlock" and recall the images formed in their minds about a particular culture group. Through observations, brainstorming, and critical analysis of a scene, the students gain insight into a culture group. Utilizing associations created in that scene, they will logically reconstruct more than 70 percent of the information about the culture and show understanding for the group's way of life. This activity may be adapted for use in studying any culture group or historical event.

PROCEDURE

Ask students to listen to and look at the presentation rather than take notes. Explain that at the end of the lesson, they must recall at least eight of the 12 ABCs of Culture in regard to the Mbuti. Suggest that they try to memorize details of the picture shown.

Display the transparency, "The Mbuti of the Rain Forest" on an overhead projector. Show the Ituri rain forest on a map to give students a sense of location. (It is mainly in the Democratic Republic of the Congo.) Tell them that the Mbuti (formerly called Pygmies) name refers to the group's self identification as "Children of the Forest" and that these are key words for the picture. Ask how might these words reflect what the Mbuti believe about themselves. ("Children" implies a dependency, and the Mbuti rely on the forest to fulfill most of their needs just as children rely on their parents.) Point to the forest in the picture and repeat the key words.

Discuss the characteristics of the Ituri rain forest environment:

- The rain forest has **varied tree heights** ranging from 30 feet to over 100 feet tall. Although you cannot see the tree tops, this can be shown by the varied widths of the tree trunks.

- There is **little vegetation under the trees** because the density of the trees blocks direct sunlight.

- There is a **lot of rainfall**. (Point to the puddles of water. Rain forests receive more than 80 inches a year; some places receive rain every day.)

RECOMMENDED TIME
- One class period

OBJECTIVES
- Draw inferences from visual materials
- Understand relationships of culture and environment

MATERIALS
- Transparency 2: "The Mbuti of the Rain Forest"
- Map showing the location of the Mbuti culture group

- Rain forests have **steady temperatures of around 80 degrees** day and night. (A warm climate is indicated by the lack of clothing the people are wearing.)

- Refer to the **woman constructing the house**. Ask the following questions about the houses:

- What is the **shape** of the house? (dome or igloo-like)

- How are the houses **constructed**? (Small branches have been placed in the ground, bent, and tied together.)

- What is the **outer covering**? (leaves to repel the water— many leaves in a rain forest have "spout-like" tips so that water runs or drips off)

- What does the **open doorway** suggest? (It does not get too cold at night, and there is trust among members of the group.)

- Are their **houses permanent**? (No, the materials will only last two or three months, which suggests the group is nomadic.)

- Why would they **not want permanent houses**? (They would have to go farther and farther away from the houses as the food supplies become depleted.)

- Relate the houses back to the term **"Children of the Forest."** (All of the materials are provided by the forest.) Stress the environmental relationships.

- Point out that only a **woman** is seen constructing the house. (social role)

Remove the picture from the screen.

Give key words and point to where the trees were located on the screen. Ask the group to relate as much information back to you as they can about the rain forest. Do the same for the houses. Replace the picture on the screen and continue.

Point to the man holding the spear and the men around the fire.

- What are examples of their **technology** from this scene? (The **spear, bow,** and **arrows** show a hunting society.)

- Speculate about the **activities around the fire**. (They are hardening the wooden tips of the arrows and applying a poison to them.)

- Point out that **only men** seem to be concerned with this activity. (social role)

- Notice the **loincloths** worn by the people. (They are made from pounding the bark of trees.)

- Ask for other signs of technology. (a **net for fishing**, a **basket**, a man smoking a **pipe**—all resources made from their environment)

Proceed to the antelope and discuss the kinds of **food** eaten by the Mbuti.

- Various types of **antelope** and **birds** found in the forest

- **Fish**, suggesting a water source nearby

- **Roots** in the basket

- **Mushrooms** and **berries** on the ground (Point out that they were gathered from the forest.)

- **Bananas** being traded from the Bantu suggesting the Mbuti trade for items not found in the forest.

Again note that a **woman is associated with the foods** gathered. (Also, all food is shared with the group.)

Remove the picture and have students start from the beginning and relate back as much information as possible.

Continue to the **man with the bananas**. Ask the students to contrast the Bantu with the Mbuti.

- The Bantu is **taller**. (Mbuti average 4'8" for the men, and 4'6" for the women; the average weight is 70 pounds. Average life expectancy is 40 years. You may wish to point out at this time that the Mbuti have a yellowish skin rather than dark due to very little exposure to direct sunlight. Mbuti also have sickle cells in their blood which are to control malaria from the mosquitoes. Mosquitoes used to live in the tops of the trees in the rain forest, but moved closer to the ground when people started cutting the trees down.)

- The Bantu is wearing **Western style clothing,** which suggests that he lives in a less isolated situation; the fabric is probably not a product of the forest.

- Speculate on what the Mbuti might trade for the bananas. (The Mbuti would probably do manual labor for the Bantu such as repairing houses of the Bantu, or would offer a portion of an animal he had killed in the forest. NOTE: the Mbuti would actually go into the Bantu village to trade, but you can justify this scene by saying this particular group camped near the edge of the forest.)

Notice the children in the picture and explore the **social roles** of the society.

- Who takes **care of the children**? (Men and women both do, and not necessarily only their own children. You may also want to speculate on what the people do for entertainment— children play hunting games and tag; adults tell stories, sing, and dance.)

- Is there a chief or **figure of authority** in the picture? (No, the Mbuti lead a cooperative existence based on group decisions. They may appoint a temporary leader or spokesperson when entering or dealing with Bantu villages, but such a person has no special privileges within the Mbuti society.)

- What are the **roles of the women**? (gather food, build the houses, and take care of the children)

- What are the **roles of the men**? (hunt, make the weapons, and take care of the children)

Remove the picture and ask questions about the mnemonic of key words; the location of features in the illustration; the significance of the items and activities featured. You might also have the class describe the Mbuti using the ABCs of Culture in the following format:

Appearance: no jewelry; loincloths made of bark; height of men 4'8"; height of women 4'6"; yellowish skin; weight of 70 pounds average

Belief system: (not illustrated on the transparency) believe in animism (everything has a soul and the power to do good or evil; believe in a supreme creator and many lesser gods; ancestors are very important)

Communication: oral rather than written tribal language; also speak languages of villagers so they may do trading; have no words in language for "jealousy" and "hate." Mbuti means "Children of the Forest."

Dates: (not illustrated) ancestors are important; events that have affected the group; births; deaths

Entertainment: sing; dance; play with children; tell stories; smoke pipes

Food: fish; antelope; birds; termites; plants from forest— mushrooms; roots; honey; food traded from villagers

Government: no chiefs except in villages; group decisions; everyone takes care of the children; little or no stealing (no doors); women gather food and build houses; men hunt and take care of weapons

Housing: dome shaped; temporary; made of saplings and leaves; no doors; cool

Information: (not illustrated) Mbuti get their education from parents and other adults; also learn from experience and from villagers

Jobs: Men are hunters; women gather food; they use spears, nets, bows, arrows, poison for arrows, baskets, and pipes, all of which are products from rain forest.

Kind of Environment: Ituri forest in the Democratic Republic of the Congo; 80 degree temperature; more than 80 inches of rain a year; shady; little vegetation on ground; three-storied trees

Leftovers: (not illustrated) Population of the Mbuti in 1938 was close to 40,000; in 1975, population was 3,800; population is declining as the rain forest is cut down and Mbuti exposed to diseases such as the common cold, to sunstroke, etc. The Mbuti, as a hunting and gathering society, will probably be extinct by the year 2000.

Extending the Activity

Organize students into groups of four or five. Have each group research and prepare a "mural method" presentation on a specific culture group.

REFERENCES

Bailey, R.C. "The Efe: Archers of the Rain Forest." *National Geographic*, November 1989, pp 664–686.

Bauer, Sam. Teacher, Lanier High School, Austin, Texas, and artist for original Mbuti mural, 1986.

Hallet, Jean-Pierre. *Pygmy Kitabu*. New York: Random House, 1973. (This book is not in print. Hallet has lived and worked with the Mbuti for many years and can be contacted through: The Pygmy Fund, Box 277, Malibu, CA 90265.)

McKenzie, Gary. Former Austin Independent School District board member who presented a workshop on using murals, from which this lesson was derived in 1986.

Putnam, Anne Eisner. "My Life with Africa's Little People." *National Geographic*, February 1960, pp. 278–302.

Putnam, John. "Yesterday's Congo, Today's Zaire." *National Geographic*, March 1973, pp. 398–432.

Thomas, Tay, and Lowell Thomas, Jr. "Flight to Adventure." *National Geographic*, July 1957, pp. 49–112.

Turnbull, Colin M. *The Forest People*. New York: Simon & Schuster, 1962.

Turnbull, Colin M. *Man in Africa*. Garden City, NJ: Anchor Books, 1977. (This book provides information on many cultural groups and includes drawings that can be used as murals.)

Cooperative Learning: Colonization of Country "X"

Creative Strategies

BACKGROUND

This activity requires students to select the appropriate location for industries, cities, farms, transportation networks, recreation areas, defense, and educational institutions within a given environment. Students use the information in their textbooks as well as a world atlas to make their decisions. Students will integrate and apply the information they have learned about climate, vegetation, and resources. There are no wrong answers but students should use logical reasoning to support their choices.

PROCEDURE

Day 1:

1. Read the following instructions to the class or write them on the board or on an overhead transparency:

Instructions:

You will be given four maps (vegetation, rainfall, elevation, and minerals) to color and a blank map on which to do your group work. These are maps of the country of "X." The student body of your school will soon colonize this area. Before settlement can begin, you, as a team of official (school) geographers, must do the following:
a. Determine the size of the population needed to settle and maintain this colony and explain why that number was chosen.
b. Locate at least three major cities on the blank map. (Name these cities and determine the sizes of their populations.)
c. Select a city for the capital. (Consider factors such as elevation, vegetation, minerals, and rainfall.)
d. Explain why you chose the cities' locations.
e. Choose a name for your country.

Each team will be working in a department of the Cabinet, planning every aspect of this new country. Each team will be given a specific assignment to cover tomorrow.

A reason *in writing* must be given for everything you do. There are few right or wrong answers in this assignment. Your reasoning for decisions is what is important, so think!

RECOMMENDED TIME
- Three class periods

OBJECTIVES
- Make logical decisions to locate human activities within a given environment
- Apply environmental data to determine population distribution

MATERIALS
- Colored pencils or markers for each student
- Handout: "Cabinet/Mission Assignments"
- Atlas for each group
- Transparency 3: "Country Description" and Transparency 4: "Map Key"
- Handout: Elevation, Minerals maps
- Handout: Vegetation, Rainfall maps
- Handout: "Country Description" with blank map for each group
- Suitable overhead transparency film for each group to create their own transparency

2. Divide the class into six teams, each representing one of the six Cabinet/Mission Assignments.

3. Have each team answer questions 1 and 2 on the handout entitled "Country Description."

4. Review the four area maps with the class:
   - Explain that the dashed lines represent boundary lines which correspond to the map legends.
   - Explain that the row of curved marks near the bottom of each map represent a fault line.
   - Remind students that one inch equals 100 miles on the map.
   - Give students a color key for the different map legends or ask them to make their own key. They may color the maps when they finish answering their questions.

Day 2:

1. Each team should locate its cities on the blank map and on the overhead transparency which they will create.

2. Remind students to use their handout maps as well as crop maps in the atlas in determining the locations of their mission activities and cities.

3. Give each team a copy of its Cabinet/Mission Assignment and make sure students answer all of the questions on their own paper.

Day 3:

1. Allow time for students to finish their work and transfer the information from their group map to their transparency.

2. Each group is to present its findings to the class by answering its Cabinet/Mission questions and giving the reasons for the selections.

3. After the presentations, tell students that the activity was designed from a satellite photograph of southeast Texas. Place the transparency key on the overhead. Point out the actual location of the major cities of this region and have students discuss this in relation to their chosen locations.

REFERENCES

Arbingast, Stanley A., et al. *Atlas of Texas*. Austin: Bureau of Business Research, The University of Texas, 1976.

Kingston, Mike, ed. *1992–93 Texas Almanac*. Dallas: Dallas Morning News, 1991.

CABINET/MISSION ASSIGNMENTS

MISSION 1: DEFENSE

1. What types of defense are needed and why?

2. Develop a key for your map showing the different types of military bases. Label them on the map. Be sure to write down your reasons for choosing the locations.

3. What type of defense do you need the most and why?

4. Is your country well suited for a space program—why or why not?

5. Don't forget to include the police as a type of defense.

6. If this was a real place, where in the world could this area be located?

MISSION 2: TRANSPORTATION

1. What types of transportation are needed and why?

2. Which areas are most in need of transportation and why?

3. What will be the main type of transportation and why?

4. Develop a key for your map showing the different types of transportation systems. Label them on the map. Be sure to write down your reasons for choosing the locations.

5. If this was a real place, where in the world could this area be located?

MISSION 3: AGRICULTURE

1. What types of crops and livestock will thrive in your colony? (Consider rainfall amount and vegetation.)

2. What will your three main crops be and why?

3. Do any of your crops require irrigation?

4. Develop a map key showing the crops that will be grown. Label the crops on the map. Make sure you grow enough food to feed the colonists. Be sure to provide reasons for locating crops in certain areas.

5. If this was a real place, where in the world could this area be located?

MISSION 4: RECREATION

1. Determine the types of recreation that can be enjoyed by everyone, young or old.

2. Develop a map key showing the types of recreation. Label them on the map. Be sure to justify your choices in writing.

3. What type of recreation can you *not* have here and why?

4. If this was a real place, where in the world could this area be located?

MISSION 5: INDUSTRY

1. Considering the country's minerals, other natural resources, and vegetation, what types of industries will you develop?

2. Locate areas where electricity can be produced.

3. Develop a map key showing the types of industries. Label them on the map. Be sure to explain in writing why the industries are located in certain places.

4. If this was a real place, where in the world could this area be located?

MISSION 6: EDUCATION

1. What types of educational facilities are needed?

2. Locate a major university that offers all subjects, as well as other universities or colleges that specialize in certain skills or knowledge needed to live and work in the country. Justify your choices in writing.

3. Locate the schools on your map.

4. Develop a map key showing educational facilities and label them on the map.

5. If this was a real place, where in the world could this area be located?

Elevation

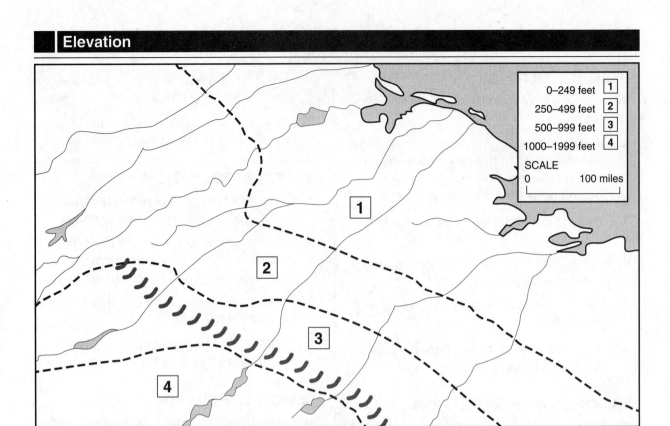

0–249 feet	1
250–499 feet	2
500–999 feet	3
1000–1999 feet	4

SCALE
0   100 miles

Minerals

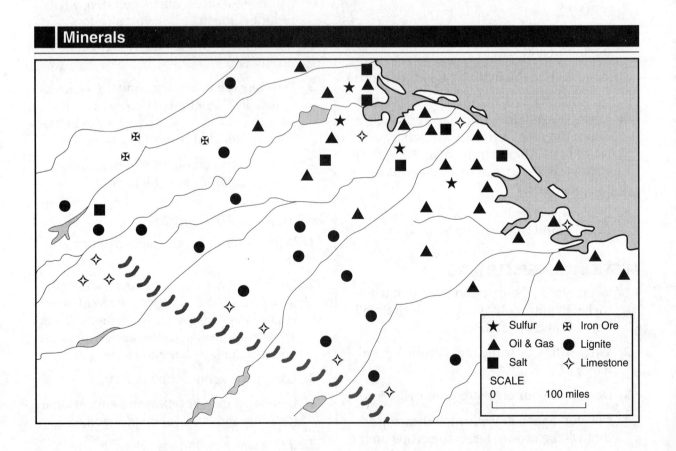

★ Sulfur   ✠ Iron Ore
▲ Oil & Gas   ● Lignite
■ Salt   ✧ Limestone

SCALE
0   100 miles

Vegetation

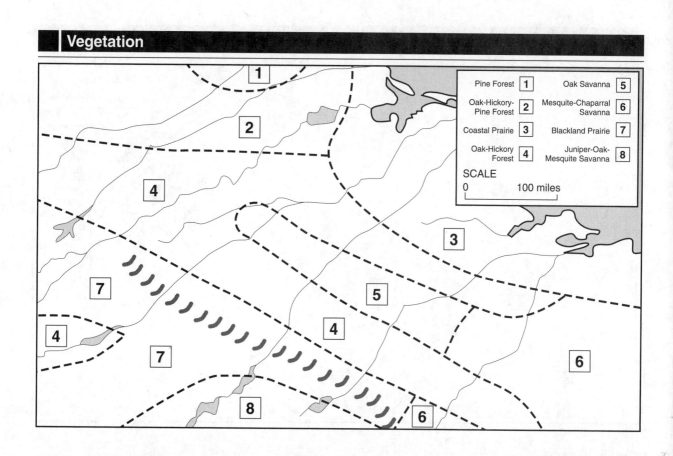

Pine Forest	1	Oak Savanna	5
Oak-Hickory-Pine Forest	2	Mesquite-Chaparral Savanna	6
Coastal Prairie	3	Blackland Prairie	7
Oak-Hickory Forest	4	Juniper-Oak-Mesquite Savanna	8

SCALE
0   100 miles

Rainfall

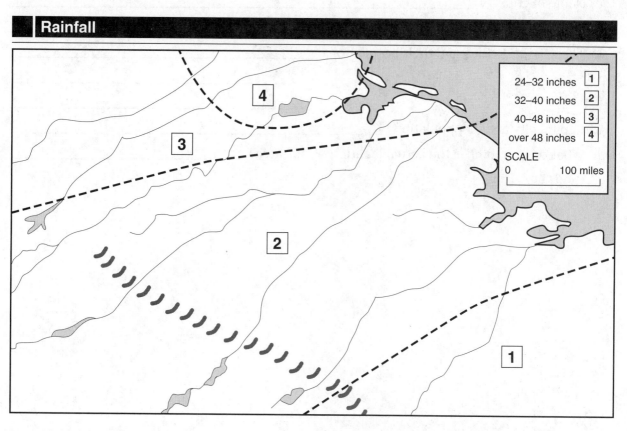

24–32 inches	1
32–40 inches	2
40–48 inches	3
over 48 inches	4

SCALE
0   100 miles

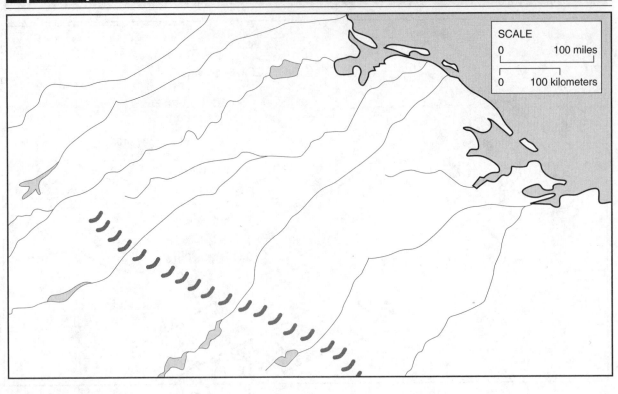

1. Name of country _____

2. Population of country _____

3. Three largest cities and their populations _____

   _____

   _____

4. Capital city and its population _____

5. What do you think is the actual location of this area? _____

Studying States Using Murals and the Themes of Geography

Creative Strategies

BACKGROUND INFORMATION

Review the Themes of Geography on page 5 of this book.

PROCEDURE

Organize the students into groups of three or four and assign each group a state to research. Explain to students that they will use their research to create a mural that illustrates the Themes of Geography which they will present to the class. One student in each group should be assigned to research one or more of the themes as it relates to the group's assigned state. Show students the transparency of Utah provided as an example of a mural they might create. Ask them to decide which pictures on the mural of Utah relate to each of the five themes. Point out that the mural of Utah illustrates the following:

Location:

absolute: 37° to 42° north latitude and 109° to 114° west longitude

relative: south of Idaho; southwest of Wyoming; west of Colorado; north of Arizona; northwest of New Mexico; east of Nevada; within the Rocky Mountain chain; in the western U.S.

Place:

physical: Great Salt Lake; Rainbow Bridge; blue spruce tree, Sego lily, beehive, seagull (state symbols); desert; Wasatch Mountains in the Rocky Mountain chain

human: 93.8% Anglo American; 4.9% Hispanic American; 0.7% African American; 1.4% Native American; 1.9% Asian American; Mormon religion; state capital—Salt Lake City

human-environment interaction: mines; skiing; beehive; building cities; camping

movement: skiing; floating on Great Salt Lake

region: Rocky Mountain chain (Explain to students that their state may comprise many regions such as desert, coastal, mountainous, and so on. Stress that region is defined by common characteristics.)

RECOMMENDED TIME
- Two or three class periods

OBJECTIVES
- Distinguish features of a state using the Themes of Geography
- Create a mural illustrating notable features of a state
- Use reference materials to acquire information

MATERIALS
- Atlas, almanacs, or other library materials that provide information on U.S. states
- Suitable paper or overhead transparency film for each group on which to create mural
- Transparency 5: "Utah"

REFERENCES

Gray, Ralph. "From Sun-clad Sea to Shining Mountains." *National Geographic Society*, April, 1964, pp. 542–91.

Leydet, Francois. "Coal Versus Parklands." *National Geographic Society*, December, 1980, pp. 776–803.

McCarry, Charles. "Utah's Shining Oasis." *National Geographic Society*, April, 1975, pp. 440–73.

Wright, John W., ed. *The Universal Almanac*. Kansas City: Andrews and McMeel, 1992.

Our Disappearing Rain Forests: What Shall We Save?

Creative Strategies

BACKGROUND

Half of Earth's rain forests have been destroyed. It is estimated that every day an area the size of six football fields disappears. Although tropical rain forests occupy only seven percent of Earth's surface, they provide a habitat for more than one-half of all of Earth's living things. Some of the consequences of worldwide rain forest destruction are listed in the student handout entitled "Rain Forest Fact Sheet."

The Amazon, the largest of the world's tropical forests, is being destroyed at an alarming rate. It is estimated that every 24 hours one million trees are cut, and that one-tenth of the Amazon rain forest has already disappeared. Amazonia makes up one-third of the world's forests, contains two-thirds of all river water, and provides one-half of the oxygen produced globally. The Amazon rain forest contains the world's greatest diversity of plant and animal species. Some scientists suggest that as many as 80,000 species have not even been classified. In fact, less than one percent of the species living in rain forests have been examined to determine their benefit to and use by humankind. According to some experts, from 50 to 70 percent of all species on earth originate in the tropics. This incredible diversity of plants and animals can only survive in their tropical environment.

This activity helps students draw conclusions about the consequences of continuing destruction of the world's rain forests. They will gain insight into the diversity and interdependence of the rain forest biome.

PROCEDURE

If time allows, have students conduct library research on Amazonia before beginning the activity. If not, provide students with background information. Possible topics for research include:

- The rate of decline of rain forests

- Reasons for destruction

- Alternatives to rain forest destruction, such as developing new uses of rain forest products

- Consequences of rain forest destruction

RECOMMENDED TIME
- One to two class periods

OBJECTIVES
- Synthesize information related to rain forest relationships
- Draw conclusions on how to save rain forests

MATERIALS
- Handout: "Rain Forest Fact Sheet" for each group
- Chart handout: "Our Disappearing Rain Forests: What Shall We Save?" for each group

- People and cultures of the rain forest
- Flora and fauna of the rain forest
- The effects of species extinction within the web of the rain forest biome
- Climatic change as a result of rain forest destruction
- Interdependencies among plant and animal species within the rain forest environment

At the start of the activity, place students in groups of three or four. Provide each group with a "Rain Forest Fact Sheet" and the chart "Our Disappearing Rain Forests: What Shall We Save?" From the Fact Sheet, each group should select the l0 items that they believe are the most important to save. They should then rank these items from 1 to 10, with number 1 being most important and number 10 least important. They will record this information on the chart, along with their reasons for saving each of the resources selected and suggestions on how this is to be accomplished.

When the groups have completed their charts, have each group present its ideas to the rest of the class, or the teacher may simply begin a discussion asking various group members to give some of their ideas. The groups will probably have some differences of opinion regarding the priority assigned to various items. You may wish to assign a student to write the student-generated ideas on the board. Then lead a class discussion directed toward arriving at a class chart, helping other students to arrive at consensus.

Extending the Activity

You may wish to have students complete a world map showing the location of the world's rain forests and their resources. The map may be constructed to show the products which are available from rain forests. Students should develop symbols representing rain forest products and place these in a map legend.

REFERENCES

Caufield, Catherine. *In the Rainforest*. Chicago: University of Chicago Press, 1984.

Cousteau, Jacques-Yves. *The Cousteau Alamanac*. New York: Doubleday & Company, Inc.: 1981.

Lewis, Scott. *The Rainforest Book*. Los Angeles: Living Planet Press, 1990.

Myers, Norman, "Rainforest: The Disappearing Forests," *Save the Earth*. Jonathan Porritt, editor, Turner Publishing, Inc., 1991.

RAIN FOREST FACT SHEET

1. Deforestation destroys habitats for rain forest wildlife. Without these large habitats, wildlife cannot breed or find sufficient food for survival.

2. The farms of the United States are affected by deforestation because many of the migrating birds that once preyed on insect pests on U.S. farms are gone. Their nesting sites in the Amazon have been destroyed. Without these birds, farmers in the U.S. lose valuable crops to the increased number of insects.

3. As a result of oil drilling in the Amazon, oil slicks are polluting the Amazon River. Oil seeps into the land and is washed into the Atlantic Ocean.

4. Deforestation results in a loss of fruits and seeds which fall from the trees of the Amazon into rivers and streams and which are an important source of food for fish. When the fish die off, the people lose an important source of protein.

5. Destruction of the rain forest has a major effect on rainfall. When trees are cleared, the hydrologic cycle is disturbed because as much as 50 percent of the rainfall in rain forests is generated by evaporation from the rain forest vegetation. Areas which have been cleared are now areas of very sparse rainfall and cannot be used in any productive way.

6. People of the rain forest depend on their environment for all their needs, both physical and spiritual. When they are deprived of their land, their entire culture is affected and possibly destroyed.

7. Curare, which comes from the bark of a liana plant, is used as a poison for arrows by people of the rain forest. It is also a valuable drug used in the treatment of multiple sclerosis, Parkinson's disease, and some muscular disorders.

8. A drug made from the tropical periwinkle plant is used to treat childhood leukemia and Hodgkin's disease, both of which are forms of cancer. Derivatives of this plant have also been shown to reduce high blood pressure. Even though only a small percentage of the plants of the rain forest have been investigated for their potential medical benefits, 7,000 plant derivatives from tropical forests are found in drugs such as those used in heart surgery, anesthetics, and many other fields.

9. Animals of the rain forest also provide valuable drugs such as anesthetics from frogs and a polio vaccine from the African green monkey.

10. Some 3,000 plants have cancer-fighting compounds; 70 percent of these plants grow in rain forests.

11. Food plants such as rice, wheat, maize, cacao (used for making chocolate) and many more originated in rain forests. Thousands of years of adaptation have given these plants genes that resist pests and disease. Modern agriculture needs these genetic aids to produce crops without the use of chemical pesticides. Cacao plantations all over the world rely on Amazon plants to provide yields and disease-resistant plants.

12. Insects cost U.S. farmers billions of dollars in crop losses. When chemical pesticides are used, the insects develop resistance, which creates the need for more powerful pesticides. But when insects from the rain forest are used to control the crop-destroying pests, the cost is far less and the crops are safer to eat.

13. The people of the rain forest are knowledgeable about medicinal plants. As these people lose their rain forest homes, their knowledge of the medicinal plants is also lost.

14. Trees of the rain forest produce products useful in industry. The rubber trees of the rain forest produce more raw materials

for rubber than trees planted in rubber plantations, and another tree produces sap that can be used as diesel fuel.

15. Worldwide weather patterns are affected by the rain forest. As rain forests absorb solar energy, atmospheric circulation affects wind and rainfall patterns world-wide. Global warming through the "greenhouse effect" also may be accelerated if rain forests are destroyed.

OUR DISAPPEARING RAIN FORESTS: WHAT SHALL WE SAVE?

The "Rain Forest Fact Sheet" lists many of the resources that will be lost, perhaps forever, if rain forest destruction continues. Refer to the fact sheet to complete the chart below. Rank in order from 1 to 10 the most important resources which you think should be saved. Number 1 should be the most important resource and number 10 the least important. In the second column, tell why you think this resource is important to save. In the third column, suggest methods for saving this resource from destruction.

	10 MOST IMPORTANT RESOURCES TO SAVE	REASONS WHY THIS RESOURCE SHOULD BE SAVED	SUGGESTED METHODS FOR SAVING THIS RESOURCE
1.			
2.			
3.			
4.			
5.			
6.			
7.			
8.			
9.			
10.			

World Geography Class Action News

Creative Strategies

BACKGROUND

Geographers have used cultural and historical geography to define a region called Middle America. Middle America includes Mexico, the seven countries of Central America, and the many islands of the Caribbean Sea. The region also includes the Isthmus of Panama, which links North America to South America. Middle America is one of the most culturally diverse regions in the world. South America extends from the warm and sunny beaches of Point Gallinas in Colombia to the cold and stormy seas around Cape Horn, about 4,500 miles to the south. Its peoples are as diverse as its physical geography. The continent's many ethnic groups are separated by geographical obstacles, including the Andes Mountains and the forests of the Amazon.

PROCEDURE

Divide the class into groups or "news teams," each having one or two anchorpersons, a weather forecaster, a sports announcer, and one or two in-the-field reporters. Assign each news team a specific country in Middle and South America. Each team will then prepare a "live news broadcast" of the country's current events.

Provide each news team a copy of the "World Geography Class Action News" handout. Allow at least two days for students to collect and organize the required information. Encourage students to be creative in the preparation of their news broadcast. Suggest using props such as illustrations, charts, graphs, maps, and so on. Direct students to almanacs, encyclopedias, and other library resources for general information on their assigned country. Tell them to consult daily newspapers for current news events, and the library's *Readers' Guide to Periodical Literature* for current magazine articles.

On the day of the "broadcast," this activity works best if a special room outside the regular classroom can be used. Some school libraries have seminar rooms where tables and desks can be arranged to simulate a news room. If possible, provide students with a microphone for their broadcasts. Again, some school libraries can provide this type of equipment. Additional learning value is added if the broadcasts are recorded on videotape. Students tend to become very serious about their work when they are being recorded. If a video camera is not available, taking slides or prints of each group is worthwhile.

RECOMMENDED TIME
- Three to four class periods

OBJECTIVES
- Explore the geography of Middle and South America through studying current events
- Develop public speaking skills
- Develop library research skills

MATERIALS
- Handout: "World Geography Class Action News" for each group
- Video camera with audio (optional)
- Microphone (optional)

WORLD GEOGRAPHY CLASS ACTION NEWS

NEWS FLASH . . .

STATION WGCAN HAS JUST BEEN CREATED WITH INTERNATIONAL NEWS UPDATES FROM AROUND THE WORLD . . .

With such distinguished reporters as:
Hugh Ups
Dan Rathernot
Warbara Balters
W.G. Ography
A.L. Atitude
and many others on the broadcast team

COLLECTIVE REPORTING EXPERIENCES INCLUDE:

Use of microphones and live videotape appearances

NEWS TEAM ASSIGNMENTS:

Teams will receive an INTERNATIONAL NEWS ASSIGNMENT.

News teams will prepare special news segments on their assigned country.

NEWS TEAM MEMBERS AND RESPONSIBILITIES:

1. **NEWS ANCHORS:** There will be two anchorpersons in each news team. Anchors are responsible for the following:
   a. prepare and broadcast current news reports
   b. design props to accompany news reports
   c. conduct interviews with foreign dignitaries
   d. announce topics to be dealt with in depth on "Nightcircle"

   Anchorpersons must report on the most recent current events occurring in their country. To find current articles, use the *Readers' Guide to Periodical Literature.* Also check for information in this week's newspapers.

2. **WEATHERPERSON:** There will be one weatherperson in each news team. The weatherperson is responsible for the following:
   a. present climate information including effects of controls of climate present in the assigned country
   b. give weather updates
   c. prepare forecasts of possible weather disturbances
   d. prepare needed props such as weather maps, charts showing high and low temperatures, etc.

   The weatherperson should discuss the types of climate found in his/her country. This should include discussion of specific controls of climate such as latitude, elevation, ocean currents, and so on. Specific information may be found in world almanacs or encyclopedias. Daily papers also frequently provide world climate information.

3. **SPORTS REPORTER:** There will be one sports reporter in each news team. The sports reporter is responsible for the following:
   a. cover local and international sports events
   b. interview sports celebrities
   c. predict the outcome of upcoming sports events
   d. discuss fitness and health issues

   The sports reporter should report on the types of sports that are popular in his/her country. General information may be found in encyclopedias and world almanacs. For current sports information the *Readers' Guide to Periodical Literature* should be used to find sports-related articles on specific countries and/or major sporting events.

4. **IN-THE-FIELD REPORTER:** There will be one or two in-the-field reporters on each news team. Their responsibilities include:

   a. report all on-the-scene disasters such as earthquakes, forest fires, etc.
   b. interview eye witnesses to major events
   c. report on the state of the environment, economy, political scene, etc.
   d. develop props to simulate the actual environment from which the news report is given

The *Readers' Guide to Periodical Literature* will provide information on natural events which have actually occurred in specific countries. In addition to actual events, the possibility of problems which are likely to occur should be reported. For example, if the country is located on the Ring of Fire, earthquakes might be a frequent concern. Other subjects for discussion could include events such as the overthrow of a government, terrorist activities, plane crashes, etc.

5. ALL REPORTERS MUST DOUBLE AS TRAVEL REPORTERS SHARING THE RESPONSIBILITY FOR GIVING INFORMATION ON TRAVEL CONDITIONS AND SIGHTSEEING IN THEIR ASSIGNED COUNTRY.

GOOD LUCK! You have two days to prepare your broadcasts. Live broadcasts begin promptly at the beginning of class on day three.

The Drama of the European Union, or Geography Students Are the Worst Hams

Creative Strategies

BACKGROUND

The European Common Market, now called the European Union (EU), is an economic union between member nations of Europe. Its basic goal is to break down barriers to trade among its member nations. The idea of this association originated with the Benelux nations in 1948. Since then, the European Union has grown to include 15 other countries of Europe.

PROCEDURE

Part of the class will briefly rehearse and present a play about the European Union. The 16 roles for the play include a narrator and representatives of the 15 members of the EU: Belgium, Denmark, France, Greece, Ireland, Italy, Luxembourg, Netherlands, Portugal, Spain, United Kingdom, Germany, Austria, Finland, and Sweden. Assign roles to students or call on volunteers. Allow time for participants to review the script before beginning. When the play is ready to begin, read the following opening remark to the class:

THE ACTION OF THIS PLAY IS AT THE HEADQUARTERS OF THE EUROPEAN UNION LOCATED IN BRUSSELS, BELGIUM. AS THE SCENE BEGINS WE HEAR FIRST FROM THE NARRATOR.

REFERENCE

Linebeck, Neal G. "Geography in the News: The Common Market." *Perspectives*. National Council for Geographic Education.

RECOMMENDED TIME

- One-half to one class period

OBJECTIVE

- Understand the purpose of the European Union

MATERIALS

- Script of play for each participant: "The Drama of the European Union, or Geography Students Are the Worst Hams"

- Badge or name card for each participant giving the name of the country represented

SCRIPT

NARRATOR:
Europe is a continent made up of many small countries. There are many different languages and ethnic groups. Although there are many natural resources in Europe, they are not distributed equally among all the different countries. In addition, these countries all have different currencies and different tax laws with restrictions on imports and exports.

If the countries of Europe all compete with each other for economic advantages, how can they compete economically on the world market?

BELGIUM:
The country of Belgium recognized this problem 30 years ago.

NETHERLANDS:
That's right. We agreed with Belgium. As early as 1948, we knew that the very small countries of Europe could not be successful on the world economic scene if we remained fragmented.

LUXEMBOURG:
That's why we joined forces with Belgium and the Netherlands to form the Benelux Economic Union.

BELGIUM:
Our union was very successful. We got rid of restrictive taxes and barriers to trade among our three countries. We established our headquarters here in Brussels, Belgium, and traded goods back and forth freely with our good neighbors of Luxembourg and the Netherlands.

FRANCE:
Yes, but you needed more natural resources to develop your industry.

GERMANY:
You certainly needed coal which, as you know, Germany has an abundance of in its Ruhr Valley.

FRANCE:
Well, don't forget, Germany, that everybody needs wheat. We have an important natural resource, too.

ITALY:
Sure, you have natural resources but what good are they without labor? Italy can supply that.

NARRATOR:
When the Benelux nations recognized that Europe would be stronger economically with the combined resources of Italy, Germany, and France, a new union was formed called the European Economic Union, or Common Market.

UNITED KINGDOM:
We recognized the advantages of the Common Market. We were reluctant, but we believe this is the best way for Europe to become powerful economically.

DENMARK:
Denmark certainly agrees!

AUSTRIA:
So does Austria. That's why we joined the European Union with Sweden and Finland in 1995.

SPAIN:
By breaking down trade barriers and allowing our diverse countries to exchange goods and labor freely across political boundaries, European countries can function like the individual states of the United States, with no trade restrictions across political boundaries.

PORTUGAL:
Right! There are no barriers to trade among the individual states of the United States. Labor and goods can be exchanged freely.

IRELAND:

The United States can combine its natural resources and labor force to build a strong economy, and Europe can do the same if our countries form an economically unified group of individual countries.

GREECE:

Don't forget, there are many problems to be faced. We don't believe that Europe, with all its diverse ethnic cultures and national histories, can blend together in a United States of Europe.

DENMARK:

You are probably right, Greece. And don't forget that Europe also has more than 10 official languages. Communication and agreement on European Union policies will not be easy.

SWEDEN:

Yes, there are problems, but we must all submerge our national egos and think of ourselves first as Europeans.

FINLAND:

If we follow Germany's advice, the European Union can become an economic giant capable of competing with the United States and Japan.

NARRATOR:

The 15 nations of the European Union include Belgium, Denmark, France, Greece, Ireland, Italy, Luxembourg, Netherlands, Portugal, Spain, the United Kingdom, Germany, Austria, Sweden, and Finland. All 15 members have agreed to band together eventually into a "unified 'Superstate,' capable of restoring Europe to the apex of world power." Meetings and discussions are still occurring today on how to accomplish this goal.

Creative Strategies

BACKGROUND

Geographers define Europe as the region stretching from the Atlantic Ocean to the Ural Mountains and from the Arctic Ocean to the Mediterranean Sea. Europe is actually the western end of the world's largest landmass, known as Eurasia. Eurasia is made up of the continents Europe and Asia. According to the theory of plate tectonics, about 300 million years ago, the two continents collided and formed the Ural Mountains at their joining. The first geography textbooks referred to Europe as the "peninsula of peninsulas." The observation is still true. While Europe contains many peninsulas of its own, it also can be viewed as a giant peninsula of Eurasia. Europe consists of more than 35 countries, some of which are among the most economically developed in the world. Several are tiny microstates, or very small countries.

PROCEDURE

Organize students into groups of three or four. Allow each group to select a European country or you may wish to assign specific countries. Give each student a copy of the instructions and review them with the class.

The purpose of this activity is to give students the opportunity to plan a vacation to a European country. Acting as travel agents from a European country, students will develop an illustrated travel brochure advertising their country as the best place for a "dream vacation." They can draw or reproduce pictures from encyclopedias, almanacs, travel books, and magazines. Travel agents often have brochures they will donate for class projects. Students may wish to telephone airlines or travel agents for additional information. If students have access to travel agents or travel guide books, have them estimate the cost of the trip. This will help them develop skills needed to arrange air flights and manage money.

Much of this activity can be completed outside of class. After each group has completed its assignment, have the class decide which brochure offers the most interesting country to visit for the best price. Display the brochures in the classroom or school library.

RECOMMENDED TIME

- Three or more class periods

OBJECTIVES

- Gain in-depth knowledge of individual countries
- Utilize resources outside the classroom
- Develop planning skills involved in overseas travel
- Practice money management skills

MATERIALS

- Handout: "Instructions for Your Dream Vacation"
- Blank 8 ½" x 11" paper for brochures
- Encyclopedias, travel books, travel brochures, and magazines
- Scissors and glue

INSTRUCTIONS FOR YOUR DREAM VACATION

You are a travel agent from the country of _____. You are competing with other travel agents in Europe to lure a large group of tourists from the United States to your country. You are to plan all aspects of the trip, from beginning to end, for the best price possible.

You must first research the places of interest and activities that are found in your country. Then decide which are the most notable and design a travel brochure for tourists. The brochure is to be created on both sides of an 8 ½" x 11" sheet of paper folded into thirds. It must include the following information:

1. climate and the best time of the year to visit the country

2. map(s) showing the country and important sites

3. places of interest with information about each

4. pictures or drawings illustrating the highlights of the trip

5. name of the currency used in the country and its value compared to the U.S. dollar

6. miles covered flying to and within the country

7. cost of round-trip airline tickets

8. an estimate of the total cost of the trip (Include such expenses as food, transportation, tips, souvenirs, and sightseeing.)

Physical Geography of Russia: Scrambled Notes

Creative Strategies

BACKGROUND

Since Russia encompasses a huge land area, there is great diversity in its physical geography. Some of the main features of Russia's environment are covered in this activity's student notes.

PROCEDURE

This activity enhances students' knowledge of Russia's physical geography while helping them develop skills in organizing information. Because the notes they are given are "scrambled," students must read and understand the information before they are able to complete the activity. For best results, have students work with partners to complete the outline. Discussion between students on proper organization of ideas may enhance learning. Since many students enjoy working with manipulative types of activities, this project is assigned as a "cut and paste" activity. Organize students into pairs and give each student the handout "Physical Geography of Russia: Scrambled Notes" and an Outline Guide. Explain to students that they will create a seven-page booklet containing important notes on Russia. Provide construction paper and have students cut this into halves or quarters. Explain that each page of the finished booklet should contain only one Roman numeral topic. That is, each Roman numeral (numbers I through VII) should be cut out of the scrambled notes and pasted on a separate page. Then they should read and decide which of the subheadings belong under each Roman numeral and its topic. Display the overhead transparency of the Outline Guide to give students an idea of how to organize the outline. After students have finished their booklets, display the overhead transparency "Outline Key" and review the correct order of the scrambled notes.

RECOMMENDED TIME
- One-half to one class period

OBJECTIVES
- Develop outlining skills
- Develop categorizing and organizing information skills
- Examine the physical geography of Russia

MATERIALS
- Handout: "Physical Geography of Russia: Scrambled Notes" for each student
- Handout: Outline Guide for each student (optional)
- Transparency 6: "Scrambled Notes Outline Guide"
- Transparency 7: "Scrambled Notes Outline Key"
- Construction paper, scissors, glue, brads

PHYSICAL GEOGRAPHY OF RUSSIA: SCRAMBLED NOTES

Instructions: The following is a scrambled outline about the physical geography of Russia. You must unscramble each outline topic and arrange it in the proper order. Create a booklet for these notes by pasting the notes on separate pieces of construction paper using one page for each of the seven Roman numerals given in the scrambled notes.

IV. WHAT ARE RUSSIA'S TEMPERATURES LIKE?

    C. There are few mountain barriers in the north to block cold arctic winds, but the Himalayas block the warm moist air from the south.

I. WHAT IS THE APPROXIMATE SIZE OF RUSSIA?

V. HOW ARE THE PEOPLE OF RUSSIA AFFECTED BY THE CLIMATE?

    A. The most northern part of Russia has a polar climate. The vegetation in this zone is *tundra*.

    B. Russia covers a huge land area and has a continental climate. Because there are many areas that do not receive the moderating effects of large bodies of water, the climate has great extremes of temperature, from very hot to very cold.

    A. Latitude affects climate because much of Russia is located in the higher (colder) latitudes.

    D. There is a large spread in latitude which also affects the range of climate.

    D. Most areas of Russia are too dry or too cold for growing crops. Most crops are grown in the steppe regions.

VI. WHAT IS THE RELATIONSHIP BETWEEN VEGETATION AND CLIMATE IN RUSSIA?

III. WHAT ARE THE MAIN FACTORS THAT AFFECT CLIMATE IN RUSSIA?

    B. Many citizens vacation in the warmest area they can find. The warmest area is located near the Black Sea where there is a Mediterranean climate.

    C. *Permafrost* in the higher (colder) regions of Russia causes many problems. People must build their houses in special ways to prevent tilting and cracking of the foundations during the summer thawing of the frozen soil.

VII. WHAT KINDS OF NATURAL RESOURCES ARE FOUND IN RUSSIA?

II. WHAT IS THE TOPOGRAPHY OF RUSSIA LIKE?

    C. Russia covers 6,000 miles from west to east and has 11 time zones.

    A. Life is difficult because the climate is so harsh. Travel is difficult, and there are very few ports that are free of ice during the long winters.

    B. The Central Siberian Plateau, located between the Yenisei and Lena rivers, has many minerals which have not been tapped.

    B. Russia has a large coastline, but it is frozen most of the year. This affects the economy because it is difficult to import and export goods.

    A. Temperatures of 30 to 40 degrees below zero are not uncommon, and it is even colder in Siberia.

    B. Winters are long and cold and the summers are short and often hot. There is little spring or fall.

B. Russia spreads over two continents, Europe and Asia.

C. The rivers of Russia are important because they provide hydroelectric power, transportation, trade, and access to the seas. However, many rivers flow north and are frozen part of the year.

A. Russia is larger than the U.S. and Mexico combined.

A. Landforms consist mainly of plains, but there are some mountains. The large number of plains affect the climate because there are no mountain ranges to block the cold winds that blow across Russia from the Arctic.

B. The subpolar climate vegetation is *taiga* which means "needleleaf forest."

C. The steppes of Russia have a dry climate, and the vegetation here is short grasses and scattered trees.

A. Russia has an abundance of natural resources, such as forests, oil and natural gas, coal, metals, and diamonds.

OUTLINE GUIDE

I. WHAT IS THE APPROXIMATE
SIZE OF RUSSIA?

   A. Russia is . . .

   B. Russia spreads . . .

   C. Russia covers . . .

II. WHAT IS THE TOPOGRAPHY
OF RUSSIA LIKE?

   A. Landforms . . .

   B. Russia has . . .

   C. The rivers . . .

III. WHAT ARE THE MAIN FACTORS THAT
AFFECT CLIMATE IN RUSSIA?

   A. Latitude . . .

   B. Russia covers a . . .

   C. There are . . .

   D. There is . . .

IV. WHAT ARE RUSSIA'S TEMPERATURES
LIKE?

   A. Temperatures . . .

   B. Winters . . .

V. HOW ARE THE PEOPLE OF RUSSIA
AFFECTED BY THE CLIMATE?

   A. Life . . .

   B. Many . . .

   C. Permafrost . . .

VI. WHAT IS THE RELATIONSHIP BETWEEN
VEGETATION AND CLIMATE IN RUSSIA?

   A. The most . . .

   B. The . . .

   C. The . . .

   D. Most . . .

VII. WHAT KINDS OF NATURAL RESOURCES
ARE FOUND IN RUSSIA?

   A. Russia has . . .

   B. The Central . . .

Creative Strategies

BACKGROUND

Review the following Controls of Climate with students:

Latitude: Generally, the higher the latitude number, the cooler the climate. The earth's climates are divided into 3 basic latitudinal belts:

> **High Latitudes:** From 60° to 90° N and from 60° to 90° S; little seasonal change; climate cool to cold year-round.
>
> **Middle Latitudes:** From 30° to 60° N and from 30° to 60° S; marked by distinct seasonal change.
>
> **Low Latitudes:** From 30° N to 30° S; little seasonal change; climate warm to hot year-round.

Elevation: Generally, the higher the elevation, the cooler the climate.

Ocean Currents: Warm ocean currents tend to produce warm, moist climates. Cold ocean currents tend to produce cool, dry climates. If a location is not near an ocean current, the effect will be minimal.

Mountains (orographic features): Mountains affect wind and rainfall patterns. Generally, rain is produced on the windward side of mountains because as the air rises, it cools and loses its ability to hold moisture.

Land Masses: Air tends to take on the characteristics of the area over which it passes. Air traveling over a warm land area will be warmed by the land. Air traveling over a cold land mass will tend to be cold. Since land heats and cools more quickly than water, air temperatures vary more (are more extreme) than air temperatures of air that has traveled over large bodies of water. Thus, regions of the world that are surrounded by large areas of land will have more extreme temperature differences ranging from very hot to very cold.

Bodies of Water: Since water heats and cools more slowly than land, large bodies of water tend to moderate climate. Regions located near large bodies of water will have a milder climate.

RECOMMENDED TIME

- Two to five class periods

OBJECTIVES

- Use climographs to visualize climate types
- Graph and interpret geographic data
- Apply and compare geographic data
- Apply knowledge about the controls of climate to understand reasons for local climates

MATERIALS

- Handout: "Climograph Questions" for each city graphed
- Handout: "Instructions for Climographs" for each student or pair of students
- Handout: "Climograph Information" for each student or pair of students
- Blank climographs, photocopied from the climograph on page 47, for each student or pair of students
- Transparency 8: "Climographs"

PROCEDURE

Have students work individually or in pairs and then review with the class the instructions for Climographs. Cover the finished sample climograph and map transparency of Almaty. Demonstrate how to plot the temperatures and precipitation on the blank climograph provided. Reveal the finished graph and map so that students can check their work later.

Many of the climograph questions can be answered from the finished climograph (see Instructions for Climographs).

Climate types for the other cities are: Moscow, Russia, humid-continental; Saratov, Russia, steppe; Kazalinsk, Kazakhstan, desert; Irkutsk, Russia, subarctic; Simferopol, Ukraine, Mediterranean; and Sagastyr, Russia, tundra.

Answers to Climograph Questions:

1. Almaty, Kazakhstan
2. Highland
3. From about 55° N to about 50° S
4. 23.5 inches
5. Forest to tundra depending on altitude
6. 15°F to 71°F
7. Cool to warm and dry (from precipitation given on climograph, summer and winter are the two driest seasons)
8. Cold and dry
9. Coffee; grain at lower altitudes
10. April, May, and June; spring; February, August, and September; summer or winter
11. Lumbering, farming, and herding
12. Because it is in the middle latitudes, it has four seasons.
13. Winter temperatures are cooler than expected at that latitude because of the elevation.
14. Continental, because temperatures are more extreme
15. Yes, because the mountains block moist air from the south
16. Elevation
17. Quito, Ecuador

REFERENCES

Pearce, E.A., and Smith, Gordon. *World Weather Guide*. New York: Random House, 1990.

Trewartha, Glenn T.; Arthur H. Robinson; and Edwin H. Hammond. *Physical Elements of Geography*. New York: McGraw-Hill Book Company, 1967.

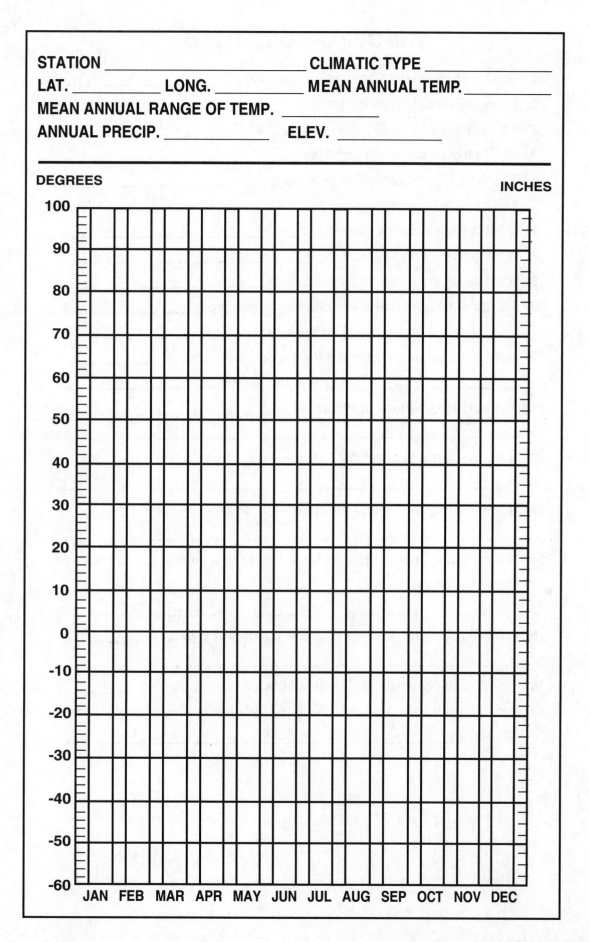

STATION _____ CLIMATIC TYPE _____
LAT. _____ LONG. _____ MEAN ANNUAL TEMP._____
MEAN ANNUAL RANGE OF TEMP. _____
ANNUAL PRECIP. _____ ELEV. _____

DEGREES   **INCHES**

100
90
80
70
60
50
40
30
20
10
0
-10
-20
-30
-40
-50
-60
   JAN FEB MAR APR MAY JUN JUL AUG SEP OCT NOV DEC

CLIMOGRAPH QUESTIONS

1. What is the name of the city and country? _____

2. Name the climate type of the city._____

3. This climate can be found in what latitudes? _____

4. The yearly rainfall of this area is _____.

5. The main type of natural vegetation is _____.

6. The average temperature range is from _____ (low) to _____ (high).

7. What is the summer climate? _____

8. What is the winter climate? _____

9. What crops are grown in this climate? _____

10. The three months that receive the most rain are _____

_____ and the season is _____. The

three months that receive the least amount of rain are _____

_____ and the season is _____.

11. What are occupations in the area? _____

_____

12. How does latitude affect the climate of this city? Explain. _____

_____

13. How does elevation affect the climate of this city? Explain. _____

_____

14. Is the climate affected mostly by a *marine* or a *continental* influence?

Explain your choice. _____

_____

15. Is the climate affected by orographic features? Explain. _____

_____

16. Which of the controls of climate affects this city the most? _____

17. Refer to your atlas to name another city and country with the same

climate. _____

INSTRUCTIONS FOR CLIMOGRAPHS

1. The TEMPERATURE figures for each month should be shown by a line graph (refer to "degrees" on the left side of each graph). Each tick mark on the temperature scale represents 2 degrees. For each month, place a red dot in the large center box above the name of the month, according to the temperature figure for that month. When all dots have been placed, connect them with a red line.

2. The PRECIPITATION figures for each month should be shown as a bar graph (refer to "inches" on the right side of each graph). Each tick mark on the precipitation scale represents .5 inch. For each month, color a blue bar above the name of the month according to the precipitation figure for that month.

3. Fill in the blank spaces at the top of each climograph according to the following instructions:

   Station: Write the name of the city and country (look up the country in your atlas).

   Climate Type: Using the latitude and longitude given with the city information, write down the name of the climate type where it is located.

   Latitude and Longitude: This is given next to the city name on the climograph information sheet.

   Mean Annual Temperature: *Add* the temperature figures for each month and divide by 12.

   Mean Annual Range of Temperature: *Subtract* the figure for the lowest temperature month from the highest temperature.

   Annual Precipitation: *Add* the precipitation figures for each month.

   Elevation: This is given next to the city name on the climograph information sheet.

4. For the CLIMOGRAPH MAP: Locate the city charted on the climograph with a red dot and print its name in red capital letters on the map. Be sure to fill in the legend. Do this for both climates represented on the two climographs.

CLIMOGRAPH INFORMATION

ALMATY 2543 ft (775 m) 43°16' N, 76°53' E

	J	F	M	A	M	J	J	A	S	O	N	D
T°	15	18	31	47	59	67	71	69	59	45	31	22
P"	1.3	0.9	2.2	4.0	3.7	2.6	1.4	1.2	1.0	2.0	1.9	1.3

MOSCOW 512 ft (156 m) 55°45' N, 37°34' E

	J	F	M	A	M	J	J	A	S	O	N	D
T°	9	15	25	42	56	61	64	63	53	43	31	20
P"	1.1	1.0	1.2	1.5	1.9	2.0	2.8	2.9	2.2	1.4	1.6	1.5

SARATOV 197 ft (60 m) 51°50' N, 45°00' E

	J	F	M	A	M	J	J	A	S	O	N	D
T°	11	13	21	43	60	69	74	69	56	42	28	17
P"	1.1	1.0	0.8	1.0	1.3	1.8	1.2	1.3	1.1	1.4	1.4	1.2

KAZALINSK 207 ft (63 m) 45°46' N, 62°06' E

	J	F	M	A	M	J	J	A	S	O	N	D
T°	11	13	26	43	64	74	78	73	62	46	30	20
P"	0.4	0.4	0.5	0.5	0.6	0.2	0.2	0.3	0.3	0.4	0.5	0.6

IRKUTSK 1,532 ft (467 m) 52°16' N, 104°19' E

	J	F	M	A	M	J	J	A	S	O	N	D
T°	−6	−2	14	31	45	56	60	58	46	31	11	−4
P"	0.5	0.4	0.3	0.6	1.3	2.2	3.1	2.8	1.7	0.7	0.6	0.6

SIMFEROPOL 673 ft (205 m) 45°01' N, 33°59' E

	J	F	M	A	M	J	J	A	S	O	N	D
T°	31	33	39	51	61	68	71	71	64	54	47	38
P"	1.8	1.5	1.6	1.1	1.5	1.4	2.5	1.5	1.4	0.9	1.7	2.1

SAGASTYR about 30 ft (9 m) 73° N, 124° E

	J	F	M	A	M	J	J	A	S	O	N	D
T°	−34	−36	−30	−7	15	32	41	38	33	6	−16	−28
P"	0.1	0.1	0.0	0.0	0.2	0.4	0.3	1.4	0.4	0.1	0.1	0.2

Contributions from the Countries of Southwest Asia and Africa

Creative Strategies

LESSON 14: *Did You Know You Were Speaking Arabic?*

LESSON 15: *Why Study Southwest Asia and North Africa?*

BACKGROUND

Many students may be unaware of the large number of contributions that emanated from the Islamic Empire, which flourished from the 7th to the 13th century A.D. This time period has been called the "Arab age of enlightenment." Through the spread of the Islamic Empire beginning in the 7th century, Arabic became the major language of large areas of Southwest Asia and North Africa. By translating Greek, Persian, and other scientific texts into Arabic and combining this knowledge with Arab scientific inquiry of the times, the Arab world made major contributions to the arts, sciences, and literature of the western world. Although many of these contributions did not come directly from Arabs or Muslims, Arabic was the "official language of learning." Thus, this rich heritage of intellectual thought includes the contributions of many ethnicities and cultures of Southwest Asia and North Africa. Three major and lasting institutions strictly of Arab origin, however, include the "university, the observatory, and the hospital." Lesson 14 examines Arabic contributions to the English language. Lesson 15 details specific contributions, such as accomplishments in the fields of medicine, music, math, and geography, and in food production.

In addition to these contributions, many items of everyday use originated in the region of Southwest Asia and North Africa.

PROCEDURE

Lesson 14: DID YOU KNOW YOU WERE SPEAKING ARABIC?

This activity makes students aware of the process of cultural diffusion. They will discover that many words they use every day derive from the Arabic language.

Organize students into teams of three or four. Give each team a list of four Arabic words. Words in the handout are divided into groups of four words each and may be cut into strips for distribution to each group of students. Note that the phonetic pronunciation of the Arabic words is approximate. There are sounds in

RECOMMENDED TIME

- One or two class periods

OBJECTIVES

- Understand the concept of cultural diffusion
- Develop writing skills
- Realize the region's contributions to western civilization

MATERIALS

- Handout/Lesson 14: List: "English Words of Arabic Origin"
- Handout/Lesson 15: (Script) "Conversations: Why Study Southwest Asia and North Africa?" for each student

Arabic for which there is no English equivalent, which explains why there might be several English spellings for one Arabic word. Each team will then write a paragraph using all of the Arabic words assigned. Paragraphs should be written in such a way that the rest of the class will be able to identify the Arabic words' English equivalent. Have a member of each group write the group's paragraph on the board or an overhead transparency. For every word identified by the class, the presenting team may receive bonus points or the equivalent of a daily grade.

Lesson 15: CONVERSATIONS: WHY STUDY SOUTHWEST ASIA AND NORTH AFRICA?

This activity, which is in the form of a "conversation" among students, provides awareness of the major contributions to western society from the region of Southwest Asia and North Africa. Give each student a copy of the script. There are 20 student parts so that almost all students in the class will have a part to read. Student number 1, however, will read several passages. You may wish to assign the parts for numbers 13 and 14 to female students since they refer to the use of cosmetics.

During the "conversations," students will list in the form of a chart the contributions of this region. You may wish to help students with this data collection by writing some of the information on the board. Charts should be titled "Contributions from Southwest Asia and North Africa" and include the following categories: Agriculture, Medicine, Music, Math, Miscellaneous, Cosmetics, Geography, and Religion. A completed sample chart is included.

REFERENCES

Boswell, Victor R.,"Our Vegetable Travelers." *National Geographic* Aug. 1949, pp. 145–217.

Introduction to the Arab World. Amideast, L. Schmida, Executive Producer, 1989.

Macron, Mary. *Arab Contributions to Civilization.* Washington, D.C.: American-Arab Antidiscrimination Committee, ADC Issues #6.

Magness, J.R. "How Fruit Came to America." *National Geographic* Sept. 1951, pp. 325–76.

"Middle East Food Production and Distribution." Austin, TX: University of Texas at Austin, Center for Middle Eastern Studies, 1984.

Mokhtari, Majib. Interviewed in Austin, Texas: September, 1993.

Panati, Charles. *Browser's Book of Beginnings: Origins of Everything Under, and Including, the Sun.* Boston: Houghton Mifflin Co., 1984.

Panati, Charles. *Extraordinary Origins of Everyday Things.* New York: Harper & Row,, 1987.

Peteet, Julie. *The Arab World in the Classroom.* "The Contributions of Arab Civilization to Mathematics and Science," Center for Contemporary Arab Studies, Georgetown University, 1985.

ENGLISH WORDS OF ARABIC ORIGIN

ENGLISH	ARABIC	PHONETIC	MEANING
safari	*safara*	sah-FAHR-rah	to travel
atlas	*atlas*	aht-LAAS	atlas
giraffe	*zirafah*	zah-RAH-fah	giraffe
gazelle	*ghazal*	gah-ZAHL	gazelle
algebra	*al-jabr*	ahl-JAAH-brr	the reduction
average	*awariyah*	ah-wahr-EE-yah	damaged merchandise
zero	*sifr*	SIEF-rr	zero
alcove	*al-qubbah*	ahl-koub-BAH	the arch
almanac	*al-manakh*	ahl-mah-NAAHK	the climate
monsoon	*mawsim*	mow-SEEM	season
typhoon	*tufan*	toh-FAHN	flood, damage
hazard	*az-zahr*	ah-ZAHR	the die
sugar	*sukkar*	souk-KAHR	sugar
mocha	*mukha*	mow-KAH	Mocha, city in Yemen
coffee	*qahwa*	kah-HWAH	coffee
lemon	*laymun*	lay-MOON	lemon
camel	*jamal*	zhay-MELL	camel
racket	*rahah*	rah-HAH	palm of the hand
magazine	*makhazin*	mahk-HAH-zeen	pl., storehouses
mummy	*mumiyah*	moo-ME-ah	mummy
cotton	*qutn*	cotton	cotton
mascara	*maskharah*	mashk-HARAH	buffoon
artichoke	*khurshuf*	khuur-SHOOF	choke of the earth
henna	*hinna*	hen-NAH	henna plant
jar	*jarrah*	jahr-RAH	jar
syrup	*sharab*	shah-RAHB	beverage, drink
sherbet	*sharbah*	shaar-BAHT	a drink
apricot	*al-birquq*	ahl-baar-KOOK	the apricot

ENGLISH	ARABIC	PHONETIC	MEANING
guitar	qitara	thay-TAHR-ah	guitar
lute	al-ud	ahl-OOD	the wood
magnet	magnatis	mag-NAH-teese	magnet
sultan	sultan	sull-TAHN	head of the union
genie	jinniy	gin-KNEE	demon
sofa	suffah	sofa	long bench
ghoul	ghul	vwhool	ghoul
gauze	qazz	cuz	raw silk
admiral	amir	ah-MERE	commander of
arsenal	dar sila' ah	dahr-SEE-lah	house of weapons
assassin	hashshashin	hahsh-SHAH-sheen	pl., users of hashish
sheik	shaykh	shake	elder, wiseman
amber	anbar	ahn-BAR	amber
alcohol	al-kuhul	ahl-KOO-houl	powdered antimony
carat	qirat	kay-RAHT	bean pod; a small weight
saffron	zafaranx	zah-fah-RAHN	bean pod; a small weight

CONVERSATIONS: WHY STUDY SOUTHWEST ASIA AND NORTH AFRICA?

STUDENT 1: I don't know why we should bother studying Southwest Asia and North Africa. I'll never go there and what does it have to do with me?

STUDENT 2: What does it have to do with you?!! Well, you eat don't you? Did you know that agriculture developed more than 10,000 years ago probably in the Fertile Crescent area where Iran, Iraq, Turkey, Syria, Israel, Lebanon and Jordan are today?

STUDENT 1: Agriculture? Big deal! I'm not a farmer. That still doesn't mean anything to me.

STUDENT 3: Some of my favorite fruits originated in this area, like pears, cherries, plums, olives, figs, dates, cantaloupe, and I just couldn't live without my apple a day.

STUDENT 4: And don't forget, we all need our veggies like carrots, artichokes, onions, broccoli, cabbage, cauliflower, asparagus, beets, parsley, celery, and my favorite, SPINACH.

STUDENT 1: Yuk! Spinach! If that's supposed to make you so strong, then why are you always missing school to go to the doctor?

STUDENT 5: Speaking of doctors, didn't you have to have stitches when you ran into the cafeteria door? Did you know that the Arabs were the first to use animal gut for stitches and antiseptics to prevent infections?

STUDENT 6: When I got stitches over my eye, my optometrist told me that Arabs pioneered ideas about how our eyes see. They were the first to develop the theory that a form or object is transmitted to the brain through the pupil of the eye.

STUDENT 7: Well, my doctor told me when I had the measles that the Arabs were the first to diagnose small pox and measles and to relate them to human contaminations. When she gave me medicine for the measles, she also told me that the first pharmacy was in Baghdad around A.D. 800. Plus, they also introduced hospitals, the idea of licensing physicians, internships and regulations about medical malpractice.

STUDENT 1: So what? That's no big deal!

STUDENT 8: Well, my father is a psychotherapist and HE said that the Arabs believed that some illnesses are psychosomatic—you know, when it's all in your mind? Some Arab physicians even had their patients delve into their subconscious to remember past events which would help to treat their illnesses. But I think the best thing is that the Arabs believed music made their patients feel better.

STUDENT 1: What does this region know about music?

STUDENT 9: We wouldn't have much of a band without the tambourine, flute, oboe, the clarinet and trumpet from Egypt, and other reed instruments from this region. And did you know even bagpipes came from there?

STUDENT 1: Enough of this talk about Southwest Asia and North Africa! I need someone to help me with my algebra homework!

STUDENT 10: Well first of all, you have to use Arabic numerals which were introduced to the world by Arab scholars. I know you are already familiar with the concept of "zero," aren't you?

STUDENT 11: Actually, the Arabs invented and developed algebra and advanced new ideas in trigonometry.

STUDENT 12: And don't forget the Egyptians who invented geometry to locate the boundaries of their farms after the Nile floods and also to build the pyramids.

STUDENT 13: Egyptians! They invented my favorite things: candy, checkers and bowling and some really useful things like beds, chairs, mirrors, glass, and eyeliner. I couldn't live without my eyeliner!

Student 14: What about lipstick, nail polish, eye shadow, perfumes, powders, hair dyes, body lotions and oils, and even wigs? The Egyptians even had beauty shops and men wore makeup too. Cosmetics were discovered in the tomb of King Tut.

STUDENT 1: You all are sure getting starry-eyed over this.

STUDENT 15: Speaking of stars, what about all the contributions to geography from this region based on the Arabs' knowledge of astronomy?

STUDENT 16: Absolute location was important in this region because of the religion. The people needed to know precise location in order to locate the holy city of Mecca, the city Muslims face when they pray.

STUDENT 17: They invented the astrolabe, an instrument used to observe the position of celestial bodies. From this they were able to determine angular measurement and thus establish precise location.

STUDENT 18: They certainly put their knowledge of location into practice when they spread their religion, Islam, from Spain to Indonesia.

STUDENT 1: It's almost lunch time, I'm going to hop into my car and get something to eat.

STUDENT 19: But wait! Without Southwest Asia and North Africa, you wouldn't have wheels for your car or coins to pay for the gas.

STUDENT 20: And did you know about all of our products that have petroleum in them? Like telephones, shampoo, toothpaste, deodorant, aspirin, clothing, shoes. . . .

STUDENT 1: STOP! STOP! I guess I should have said what **doesn't** come from Southwest Asia and North Africa?

CONTRIBUTIONS FROM SOUTHWEST ASIA AND NORTH AFRICA

Agriculture	Medicine	Music	Math	Miscellaneous	Cosmetics	Geography	Religion
1. Developed farming 2. Fruits: pears, cherries, plums, olives, figs, dates, cantaloupes, apples 3. Vegetables: carrots, artichokes, onions, broccoli, cabbage, cauliflower, asparagus, beets, parsley, celery, spinach	1. Animal gut for stiches 2. Antiseptics to prevent infections 3. Theory that an object is transmitted to the brain through the pupil of the eye 4. Diagnosed small pox and measles 5. First pharmacy 6. First hospitals 7. Licensing of physicians 8. Internships for physicians 9. Regulations about medical malpractice 10. Psychosomatic illnesses 11. Had patients delve into subconscious to remember past events 12. Music to make patients feel better	1. Instruments: tambourine, flute, oboe, clarinet, trumpet, bagpipes	1. Arabic numerals 2. Concept of "zero" 3. Algebra 4. New ideas in trigonometry 5. Geometry	1. Candy 2. The game of "checkers" 3. Bowling 4. Beds 5. Chairs 6. Mirrors 7. Glass 8. Wheel 9. Coins	1. Eyeliner, lipstick, nail polish, eye shadow, perfumes, powders, hair dyes, body lotions, and oils 2. Wigs 3. Beauty shops	1. Astrolabe (to determine latitude)	1. Islam

Creative Strategies

BACKGROUND

This activity helps dispel some of the preconceived ideas and stereotypes about Africa frequently held by students. Each of the questions on the student handout reflects a commonly held misconception people believe to be true about Africa; however, all but the first statement are false. You will find that most students will incorrectly respond with more true than false answers, illustrating how common these misconceptions are in our society.

The necessary background information is found in the answers provided. You can use this activity as a model to dispel stereotypes about any region in the world.

PROCEDURE

Give each student a copy of "How Much do You Know About Africa?" Explain that this is not a quiz that will be graded, but is only a general guideline to determine their knowledge about Africa. Tell them to guess if they do not know an answer. They should write down the number of TRUE statements on the bottom of the page and turn the paper over when they are finished. Most students will finish in about 10 minutes. Ask students to raise their hands if they found 11 to 16 true statements, 6 to 10, 5 or less. Initiate a lively class discussion by telling students that number one is the only true statement. As each statement is discussed, have students underline the word(s) that make it false and write the appropriate corrections under each.

Answers:

1. The U.S. (3,618,765 square miles) fits into Africa (11,688,000 square miles) about 3.2 times.

2. Africa is actually about 55% savanna grassland, 25% desert (and increasing in size), and 10% rain forest (and decreasing in size). The "jungle"—very thick vegetation—is usually found only around rivers where the sun can penetrate the canopy of the rain forest trees. Natural rain forests have little ground vegetation due to the blockage of the sun by the trees.

3. There are no tigers in Africa. Less than 1% of the animal population Africa had in 1900 remains today due to poaching and human encroachment into wildlife habitats.

RECOMMENDED TIME

* One or two class periods

OBJECTIVE

* Develop awareness of the myths and stereotypes about Africa

MATERIALS

* Handout: "How Much do You Know About Africa?" for each student

4. There are over 700 different culture groups in Africa.

5. There is very little seasonal change in Africa due to its tropical location. Ninety percent of Africa is located within the tropics. Seasonal change in most of Africa consists of a wet and a dry season.

6. Africa is a *continent* with more countries than any other continent.

7. The Afro is a hair style that originated in the United States.

8. See number 4.

9. Nearly every African country has experienced political problems related to ethnic or tribal differences. For example, the issue of leadership has been disputed in Uganda, Nigeria, Angola, Ethiopia, Sudan and Somalia.

10. Africa has a vast amount of resources: 70% of the world's diamonds, 60% of the world's gold, 40% of the world's water power, in addition to copper, tin, platinum, uranium, and more.

11. Africans live in all types of houses. The term "hut" came from the ethnocentrism of European colonizers.

12. The female lion does most of the hunting. "King of the Jungle" should actually be "Queen of the Savanna!"

13. Africans had many advanced civilizations, but few written records survived. Many African societies have a rich oral history which was not recognized by European societies.

14. The Nile is the *longest* river in the world; the Amazon is the largest in water volume.

15. Most Africans speak their tribal language, another tribal or regional language (such as Swahili in East Africa), and a European language.

16. Explain to your students that everyone is a "native" of some place and that the term should not apply only to Africans. There are also people of many ethnicities, such as Arabs and Asians, who are natives of Africa.

REFERENCES

Davidson, Basil. *Africa in History*. New York: Collier Books, 1991.

July, Robert W. *A History of the African People*. New York: Charles Scribner's Sons, 1992.

Oliver, Roland and J.D. Fage. *A Short History of Africa*. Baltimore: Penguin Books, 1988.

Turnbull, Colin M. *Man in Africa*. Garden City: Anchor Books, 1977.

HOW MUCH DO YOU KNOW ABOUT AFRICA?

Instructions: Answer the following statements by writing True or False in the space provided.

_____ **1.** The land area of the United States fits into the land area of Africa a little over three times.

_____ **2.** Africa is composed mostly of desert, jungle, and some grassland.

_____ **3.** Africa has lions, tigers and many other wild animals.

_____ **4.** The cultures of Africa are very similar.

_____ **5.** Most of Africa experiences four seasons each year.

_____ **6.** Africa is one of the largest countries in the world.

_____ **7.** The "Afro" is a hair style from Africa.

_____ **8.** There are very few tribes left in Africa today.

_____ **9.** Outside of South Africa, there are very few ethnic problems in Africa.

_____ **10.** Africa is a poor land with few resources.

_____ **11.** The people in Africa live in huts.

_____ **12.** The male lion is the best hunter of all the African cats.

_____ **13.** Africa had no early history or any advanced civilizations.

_____ **14.** The largest river in the world is the Nile.

_____ **15.** Most Africans speak the same language.

_____ **16.** Africans are either natives or Europeans.

_____ Write down your total number of TRUE statements.

Exploring Culture Through Language:
African Charades

Creative Strategies

BACKGROUND

In East Africa, the Swahili language developed as a result of the blending of the African Bantu language with many foreign words. Cultural diffusion played a major role. Because of East Africa's contact with Arab traders, Swahili was originally written using the Arabic alphabet and adopted many Arabic words. With colonialism, the language acquired many other foreign words. It has now become an almost universal language throughout East Africa. Because language reflects culture, an understanding of some Swahili words and proverbs can provide students with many insights into East African culture. In addition, a comparison between the students' own culture and the cultures of Africa helps lessen the ethnocentrism students often display when exposed to other cultures.

A unique way Africans have incorporated Swahili words and proverbs into everyday life is by displaying them on their clothing. The *kanga* is a simple garment consisting of a single piece of cloth approximately 64 inches by 45 inches (163 cm by 114 cm), worn in a variety of styles. African proverbs appear as part of the design of the *kanga*. *Kangas* are often given as presents, husband to wife or from one friend to another. They are worn by men as sleeping garments and are worn virtually all the time by women. One of the most common uses of the *kanga* is as a carrier for an infant. The *kanga* is simply folded into a sling worn on the mother's back. Babies in Africa usually accompany their mothers everywhere, from work in the fields to shopping and completing of daily chores.

Pronunciation for Swahili words is straightforward except for the (um) sound. This sound is a distinct syllable made with closed lips but with a slight "u" sound beforehand. There is no "u" sound when the "m" precedes a "w."

PROCEDURE

Organize students into groups of four. Make cards (from information on handouts) and give each group a card containing a Swahili word or proverb with its pronunciation on one side, and the literal translation and (for the proverbs) the English counterpart given on the reverse. Each group in turn writes its own

RECOMMENDED TIME

- One or two class periods

OBJECTIVES

- Analyze culture traits
- Learn about East African cultures through the use of African proverbs and the Swahili language
- Compare similarities among cultures

MATERIALS

- Handout: "Swahili Proverbs"
- Handout: "Swahili Words"
- Transparencies 9–12: "Ways to Wear a *Kanga*"
- Kangas (if available) or strips of fabric approximately 64" x 45" (optional)
- Culturgrams (see book listed in References, page 64)

Swahili word or proverb on the chalkboard, pronounces the word(s) for the class and then proceeds to "act out" the literal meaning, as in the game of charades. The class attempts to guess what English word is being described; for the proverbs, the class should then try to guess the proverb's conceptual meaning or English counterpart. If acting out one of the proverbs, students should model the exact Swahili saying. The class must try to guess the proverb and then they may relate this to a similar proverb from their own culture. Note that some of the words given here reflect specific culture traits such as beliefs or values or special life events as practiced in African societies. To reinforce the elements of culture, students may be asked to categorize each word using the ABCs of Culture. (See Lesson 4, *Creative Strategies for Teaching World Geography*, pages 9–10)

The following ideas should be discussed as part of this activity:

1. *Basic human needs and concerns are reflected through language in all cultures.*

2. *Cultures share universal ideas of behavior and social mores.*

3. *Language provides insight into adaptation to different environments and reflects human-environment interaction.*

Extending the Activity #1: Have student groups conduct further research about the culture trait reflected by their card. Each group may then present this additional information to the rest of the class. An excellent resource for the groups' research may be found in a series of "Culturgrams" available in many school libraries.

Extending the Activity #2: Students may wish to create their own *kangas* either on butcher paper or by using old sheets. They can create their own designs, use their favorite proverbs, or create an original proverb that represents their own value systems.

REFERENCES

Culturgrams for the 90's. Grant Paul Skabelund, ed. Provo, Utah: Brigham Young University, David M. Kennedy Center for International Studies Publication Services, 1990.

Feelings, Muriel, and Tom Feelings. *Jambo Means Hello.* New York: Dial Books for Young Readers, 1974.

Hanby, Jeanette, and David Bygott. *Kangas: 101 Uses.* Nairobi, Kenya: Ines May Publicity, 1984.

Mucheru, Grace, and John Mucheru. Interviewed in Nairobi: July, 1993.

Salim, Ahmed Ali. *Living Swahili: A Complete Language Course.* New York: Crown Publishing, Inc., 1971.

SWAHILI PROVERBS

1. *Udongo upate ulimaji.*
   oo-DOEN-go oo-PAH-tay oo-lee-MAH-gee
   Get the mud while it is still wet.
   (Strike while the iron is hot.)

2. *Nazi mbovu harabu ya nzima.*
   NAH-zee (um)-BOW-voo hah-RAH-boo
      YAH NZEE-mah
   A bad coconut spoils the good ones.
   (One bad apple spoils the barrel.)

3. *Asiyekuwapo na lake halipo.*
   ah-see-yeah-koo-WAH-poe NAH LAH-kay
      hah-LEY-poe
   **He who is not there, nothing of his is
      there.**
   (Out of sight, out of mind.)

4. *Penye nia pana njia.*
   PENH-yeah NEE-ah PAH-nah NGEE-ah
   Where there is a will, there is a way.
   (Where there is a will, there is a way.)

5. *Kawia ufike.*
   kah-WEE-ah oo-FEE-kay
   Be late but get there.
   (Better late than never.)

6. *Moja shika si kumi nenda uje.*
   MOE-jah SHE-kah SEE COO-me NAYN-dah
      OO-jay
   **The one you are holding is better than
      the ten you are hoping for.**
   (A bird in hand is worth two in the bush.)

7. *Haraka haraka haina baraka.*
   hah-RAH-kah hah-RAH-kah hah-EE-nah
      bah-RAH-kah
   Hurry, hurry has no blessing.
   (Haste makes waste.)

8. *Mwana umleavyo ndivyo akuavyo.*
   MWAH-rah oom-lay-ah-VEE-oh DEEV-yoe
      ah-koo-ah-VEE-oh
   **The way you bring up a child, that is
      the way he will be.**
   (As the twig is bent, so grows the tree.)

9. *Mtoto wa nyoka ni nyoka.*
   (um)-TOE-toe wah NYOE-kah NEE
      NYOE-kah
   A baby of a snake is a snake.
   (Like father, like son.)

10. *Bendera hufuata upepo.*
    ben-DAIR-ah who-foo-AH-tah oo-PAY-poe
    The flag follows the wind.
    (Go with the flow.)

11. *Ulimi hauna mfupa.*
    oo-LEE-mee hah-OO-nah (um)-FOO-pah
    The tongue has no bone.
    (The bark is worse than the bite.)

12. *Adhabu ya kaburi aijuaye ni maiti.*
    ah-TAH-boo YAH kah-BOO-ree
       aye-JEW-aye NEE mah-EE-tee
    **He who knows the torment of the grave
       is the corpse.**
    *(Never judge a person until you have
       walked a mile in his shoes.)*

13. *Vita havina macho.*
    VEE-tah hah-VEE-nah MAH-choh
    War has no eyes.
    (War spares no one.)

14. *Maneno mema humtoa nyoka pangoni.*
    mah-NEE-noe MAY-mah whom-TOE-ah
       NYOE-kah pahn-GOEN-ee
    **Kind words attract the snake out of its
       hiding place.**
    *(It is easier to catch flies with honey than
       with vinegar.)*

15. *Mtaka cha mvunguni sharti ainame.*
    (um)-TAH-kah CHAH (um)-voon-GOO-nee
       SHAHR-tee aya-NAH-meh
    **If you want something under the bed,
       you have to bend.**
    (You can't get something for nothing.)

16. *Mpanda ngazi hushuka.*
    (um)-PAHN-dah NGAH-zee who-SHEW-kah
    **The person that climbs on a ladder
       must come down.**
    (Whatever goes up, must come down.)

17. *Maji yakimwagika hayazoleki.*
    MAH-gee yah-key-mwah-GHEE-kah ha-
       yah-zoe-LAY-key
    Spilled water can never be picked up.
    (It's no use crying over spilled milk.)

18. Paka akiondoka panya hutawala.
PAH-kah ah-key-ohn-DOE-kah PANH-yah
    WHO-tah WAH-lah
When the cat leaves, the rat rules.
(When the cat is away, the mice will play.)

19. Mcha mwana kulia hulia yeye.
(UM)-cha MWAH-nah coo-LEE-ah who-
    LEE-ah YEAH-yeah
**He who fears his child's crying will cry
    himself.**
(Spare the rod and spoil the child.)

20. Dalili ya mvua ni mawingu.
dah-LEE-lee YAH (um)-VOO-ah NEE ma-
    WEEN-goo
The sign of the rains is the clouds.
(Where there is smoke, there is fire.)

21. Dawa ya moto ni moto.
DAH-wah YAH moe-TOE NEE MOE-toe
A cure for fire is fire.
(Fight fire with fire.)

22. Kamba hukatikia pabovu.
KHAM-bah who-kha-tee-KEY-ah
    pah-BOW-voo
**Rope usually breaks at its weakest
    point.**
*(A chain is only as strong as its weakest
    link.)*

**23. Nahodha wengi jahazi huenda
    mrama.**
nah-HOE-dah WHEN-gee jah-HAH-zee
    who-AYN-dah (um)RAH-mah
**Too many captains will make the boat
    capsize.**
(Too many cooks spoil the broth.)

24. Akufaaye kwa dhiki rafiki.
ah-koo-FAAH-yeah KWAH THEE-key rah-
    FEE-key
**He who rescues you in time of need is
    indeed a friend.**
(A friend in need is a friend indeed.)

25. Haba na haba hujaza kibaba.
HA-bah NAH HAH-bah who-JAH-zah key-
    BAH-bah
Little by little fills the measure.
(A journey begins one step at a time.)

SWAHILI WORDS

ENGLISH	SWAHILI	PRONUNCIATION
wedding	*arusi*	ah-ROO-see
food	*chakula*	cha-KOO-lah
farm	*shamba*	SHAM-bah
hello	*jambo*	JAHM-bow
freedom	*uhuru*	oo-WHO-roo
welcome	*karibu*	kaa-REE-boo
friend	*rafiki*	rah-FEE-key
drum and dance	*ngoma*	n-GO-mah
cow, cattle	*ngombe*	n-GOM-bay
school	*shule*	SHOE-lay
shop	*duka*	DEW-kah
farmer	*mkulima*	(um)koo-LEE-mah
herder	*mchungaji*	(um)choon-GAH-gee
love	*upendo*	oo-PEN-doe
fisherman	*mvuvi*	(um)VOO-vee
student	*mwanafunzi*	mwah-nah-FOON-zee
teacher	*mwalimu*	mwah-LEE-moo
country	*nchi*	N-chee
city	*mji*	(UM)-gee
house	*nyumba*	NYOOM-bah
clothes	*nguo*	n-GOO-oe
religion	*dini*	DEE-nee
ancestor	*mkale*	(um)-KAH-lay
thank you	*asante*	ah-SANH-tay
chair	*kiti*	KEY-tee
river	*mto*	(UM)-toe
mountain	*mlima*	(um)-LEE-mah
medicine	*dawa*	DAH-wah
lion	*simba*	SEEM-bah
giraffe	*twiga*	TWEE-gah

Creating an Asian Holiday Calendar

Creative Strategies

BACKGROUND

This activity is designed to acquaint students with a variety of culture traits practiced by the people of Asia. The universals of culture are often revealed in festivals, holidays, and other celebrations. For example, celebration of the Rice Festival in Japan reveals Japanese attitudes about religion, social roles, and types of music and dance. During the rice festival, rituals associated with prayers to the Rice God are performed by women. Work in the fields during the transplanting of rice seeds is highly organized to the music of drums and pipes. The holiday *Quing Ming,* meaning "Bright and Clear," reveals Chinese reverence for ancestors. *Quing Ming* is a happy occasion when people visit graves to clear away the weeds and make offerings of wine and food to the departed spirits of their ancestors. Cultural diffusion is also evident in some Asian celebrations, although Asia's rich tapestry of ethnicity provides an amazing diversity of beliefs and practices.

PROCEDURE

Give each student a copy of the instructions for creating an Asian Holiday Calendar. Then organize students into groups of three or four. Students will spend at least one class period in the library conducting research on Asian holidays. They should work co-operatively, sharing responsibilities for collecting information. After students have completed their research, provide each group with construction paper or any other paper suitable for drawing pictures and 12 blank calendar pages. When students complete their calendars, you may wish to initiate a discussion of culture traits such as religion, social roles, economy, and the other ABCs of Culture that are reflected in the holidays of various Asian countries.

REFERENCE

Van Straalen, Alice. *The Book of Holidays Around the World.* New York: E.P. Dutton, 1986.

RECOMMENDED TIME

- Two to four class periods

OBJECTIVES

- Gain insight into the cultures of Asia
- Develop writing skills
- Develop library research skills
- Reinforce knowledge of the ABCs (universals) of Culture

MATERIALS

- Handout: "Instructions: Constructing an Asian Holiday Calendar" for each student
- Paper and art materials for each group
- Handout: blank calendar pages for each group
- Library reference materials

INSTRUCTIONS: CONSTRUCTING AN ASIAN HOLIDAY CALENDAR

Members of your group should work together to divide responsibilities and share information. Use library resources such as encyclopedias, *National Geographic, Readers' Guide to Periodical Literature,* the card catalog, and almanacs to create an Asian Holiday Calendar.

1. Locate information about 12 or more holidays that are celebrated in various countries of Asia. You may choose one or more holidays for each month from at least four of the countries listed below.

   China
   Indonesia
   Laos
   Mongolia
   Vietnam
   North Korea
   Myanmar (Burma)
   Cambodia (Kampuchea)

   Japan
   Malaysia
   Thailand
   Philippines
   Taiwan
   South Korea

2. Read about the holidays and take notes to be used when preparing your calendar. Be sure to include information on why this holiday is celebrated. For example, it may be a religious holiday, a national holiday, a wedding, New Year's, or another celebration.

3. Begin construction of your calendar. You will need 12 sheets of blank paper for your illustrations and 12 blank calendar pages.

4. Fill in each calendar page with the name of the month, days of the week, and the dates. Be sure to list the specific holidays you have chosen in the box where the date appears. You may wish to conduct additional research so that you can list months and dates in an Asian language or script.

5. On each of your 12 blank sheets of paper, draw an illustration that represents the holidays you have chosen. Beneath each picture, write an explanation of the holiday illustrated.

Creative Strategies

BACKGROUND

The art of origami is an important aspect of much of Japanese culture. When paper was introduced to Japan from China in the sixth century, it was valued even above silk for Japanese drawing. *Origami*, which means literally "folded paper," became a specialized art form.

The use of origami as a pastime for children began in the 14th century. However, it was mainly considered appropriate for young girls because it was believed that paper-folding helped train them for their future responsibility of sewing. By the 20th century, there were approximately 150 standardized types of origami, such as cranes and other animal forms, used by children. Origami was made a part of the school curriculum on the premise that it provided training for young minds in the principles of plane geometry. Tokyo now boasts the Origami Research Center.

Today origami is used in a variety of ways that reveal Japanese reverence for paper and paper-folding and its religious significance. For example, folded paper might be placed near a sacred shrine. Shinto priests use sticks containing large amounts of folded paper in rites of purification. In rites of exorcism, a folded paper is used to represent the soul of the possessed person. The paper is said to absorb the evil spirits after which it is set ablaze and sent away on the currents of a river. In Hiroshima, a memorial to the dead features a display consisting of many separate strings of 1,000 origami cranes each. These paper offerings carry a blessing for the souls of the dead. Cranes are also associated with good luck. Often given as gifts to people who are ill, they bring a wish for good luck and a prayer for recovery. Origami is also part of Japanese celebrations, such as the wedding ceremony.

PROCEDURE

Through class discussion, tell students about the Japanese art of origami. Relate this art form to Japanese culture traits, such as reverence for the beauty of nature. Origami most often shows elements of nature such as birds and insects. Display the transparency showing the origami figure of a swan. Explain that

RECOMMENDED TIME
- One or two class periods

OBJECTIVES
- Explore Japanese culture through art
- Create a form of Japanese art

MATERIALS
- Enough six-inch squares of various types of paper for each student
- Transparency 13: "Origami"
- Coat hangers and string for building mobiles (optional)

Shintoism, one of the religions of Japan, stresses harmony with nature and uses origami in religious rites. Perfection of art is also stressed in Japan and is reflected in the training of children in origami. Provide students with books on Japanese origami that include instructions on how to make a variety of origami figures. Then provide students with colored paper (gift wrap works well for some designs). The standard size of paper for origami is 15 square centimeters (about six inches); however, any kind or size paper may be used as long as the paper is cut into a square. Another rule which must be strictly followed is that origami figures may not be cut or colored after folding is completed.

Students may work individually or in groups to complete their assignments. An interesting way to display student work is by building mobiles using coat hangers.

Extending the Activity
You may wish to have students conduct additional research on Japanese arts and relate each item studied to selected "ABCs of Culture" (Lesson 4, pages 9–10)

REFERENCES

Dalby, Liza, et. al. *All Japan: The Catalogue of Everything Japanese.* New York: Quill, 1984.

Honda, Isao. *The World of Origami.* New York: Japan Publications Trading Company, 1965.

Takahama, Toshie. *Origami for Fun.* Tokyo: Shufunotomo Co., Ltd., 1985.

Creative Strategies

BACKGROUND

South Asia, sometimes called the Indian subcontinent, is a large triangular peninsula that juts into the Indian Ocean. The region is one of physical extremes. Barren deserts contrast with flooded river deltas and tropical islands. The world's highest mountains rise up in the north, earning this area the nickname "the roof of the world." South Asia is a region of great cultural contrasts as well. More than one-fifth of the world's people live on the South Asian peninsula. The region's long cultural history has resulted in a mixture of religions, languages, and other culture traits. In recent decades, South Asia has continued to experience high population growth, increased stress on the environment, and many economic changes.

PROCEDURE

Laminate the Bingo Question and Answer Cards (clear contact paper works well) and cut apart. During play, have a student shuffle the cards so that the questions are asked at random.

Give each student one blank Bingo Card and the handout of answers. Display the overhead transparency provided. Explain that students are to write 24 answers on their cards, or one answer in each square on the card. Ask students to select any 24 answers from the list shown. Be sure to collect Bingo answer sheets before beginning the game so that students cannot change their selected answers in order to win. Explain that the same Bingo Card will be used for all games played. When marking correct answers they should write a small number 1 for the first game, a small number 2 for the second, and so on.

After the Question and Answer Cards have been shuffled, read each question to students. If a student has the correct answer, he/she marks the Bingo Card appropriately. Allow students to use their textbooks and especially the map of South Asia on page 559 to find answers since all questions are taken directly from the textbook. This helps prevent students from becoming disinterested if they do not know the answers. The game might also be played as a team activity. In addition, small prizes or points might be awarded to stimulate student interest and participation.

RECOMMENDED TIME
- One class period

OBJECTIVES
- Review factual information

MATERIALS
- Handout: "Answers to South Asia: Bingo"
- One set of Bingo Question and Answer Cards
- Handout: Blank Bingo Cards (one or more for each student)
- Transparency 14: "South Asia Bingo"

ANSWERS TO SOUTH ASIA BINGO

Instructions: Select any 24 answers from the list below and write them in the blanks on your Bingo Card. When a question is called, make a mark on your card if you have written in the correct answer. To use your card for more than one game, mark a small number 1 for a correct answer for the first game, a small number 2 for the second game, and so on.

1. subcontinent
2. India, Pakistan, Nepal, Bhutan, and Bangladesh
3. Nepal and Bhutan
4. Maldives
5. Sri Lanka
6. Gondwanaland
7. Himalaya
8. Hinduism
9. Sikhism
10. Great Britain
11. Taj Mahal
12. Bangladesh
13. Deccan
14. Indo-Gangetic
15. Thar
16. Cambay
17. Eastern and Western Ghats
18. monsoons
19. Bay of Bengal
20. Arabian Sea
21. Gulf of Mannar
22. Male
23. New Delhi
24. Dhaka
25. Kathmandu
26. Thimphu
27. Colombo
28. Islamabad
29. calico
30. Mount Everest
31. tropical cyclones
32. storm surge
33. 2
34. 900
35. 15
36. deforestation
37. 70
38. farming
39. *sari*
40. caste system
41. Mohandas Gandhi
42. 25
43. Calcutta
44. Bombay
45. tea, coffee, cashews and tobacco
46. hydroelectric power
47. cottage industries
48. Hindi
49. Dravidian
50. English
51. democracy
52. Indira Gandhi
53. Ganges
54. Karakoram
55. desert
56. Islam

BINGO QUESTION & ANSWER CARDS

Q: Because South Asia forms a large triangular peninsula jutting into the Indian Ocean, it is sometimes called a _____.

A: subcontinent

Q: _____ and _____ are countries located in the mountain rim north of India.

A: Nepal and Bhutan

Q: Mainland South Asia is made up of the countries of _____, _____, _____, _____, and _____.

A: India, Pakistan, Nepal, Bhutan, and Bangladesh

Q: Name the tropical islands located southwest of Sri Lanka in the Indian Ocean.

A: Maldives

Q: The relative location of _____ is southeast of the southern tip of the India.

A: Sri Lanka

Q: _____ is the major religion of India.

A: Hinduism

Q: Geographers believe that India was once a part of the southern supercontinent called _____.

A: Gondwanaland

Q: The religion practiced in India that is a blend of Hindu and Muslim teachings is _____.

A: Sikhism

Q: When the Indian subcontinent drifted north and slammed into Eurasia, the _____ mountains were formed.

A: Himalaya

Q: The European country that took control of India in the 18th century and ruled until 1947 was _____.

A: Great Britain

Q: One of the world's most beautiful buildings is a tomb built for the wife of one of India's past rulers. This landmark in Agra, India, is called the _____.

A: Taj Mahal

Q: Name the plains of northern India stretching from the Arabian Sea to the Bay of Bengal.

A: Indo-Gangetic

Q: When East Pakistan broke away from West Pakistan, the nation of _____ was formed.

A: Bangladesh

Q: The name of the desert located in northwest India is the _____.

A: Thar

Q: Name the plateau located in the south central part of India.

A: Deccan

Q: The Narmada River flows into the Gulf of _____.

A: Cambay

Q: These hills are located on both the eastern and western edges of the Deccan Plateau.

A: Eastern and Western Ghats

Q: The relative location of this large body of water is west of India and east of Saudi Arabia.

A: Arabian Sea

Q: The climate and rainfall patterns of India are greatly influenced by seasonal winds called _____.

A: monsoons

Q: The body of water separating southern India and Sri Lanka is the _____.

A: Gulf of Mannar

Q: The relative location of this large body of water is east of India and south of Bangladesh. It is the _____.

A: Bay of Bengal

Q: The capital of the Maldives is _____.

A: Male

Q: The capital of India is
____.

A: New Delhi

Q: The capital of Bhutan is
____.

A: Thimphu

Q: The capital of Bangladesh is
____.

A: Dhaka

Q: The capital of Sri Lanka is
____.

A: Colombo

Q: The capital of Nepal is
____.

A: Kathmandu

Q: The capital of Pakistan is
____.

A: Islamabad

Q: Name the cotton fabric that was important to the Indian economy in the 1600s.

A: calico

Q: A rise in sea level resulting from a tropical cyclone is called a _____.

A: storm surge

Q: Name the tallest mountain in the Himalayas.

A: Mount Everest

Q: India's population increases about _____ percent per year.

A: 2

Q: Bangladesh is frequently struck by severe storms called _____.

A: tropical cyclones

Q: The population of India is more than _____ million.

A: 900

Q: At its present growth rate, India's population grows by more than _____ million people per year.

A: 15

Q: The occupation of most Indian people is _____.

A: farming

Q: _____ causes a loss of valuable forest resources, destroys wildlife habitats and causes flooding and soil erosion.

A: deforestation

Q: Many Indian women wear a garment called a _____.

A: *sari*

Q: People living in rural areas make up _____ percent of South Asia's population.

A: 70

Q: The social ranking begun by Hindu Aryans is called the _____.

A: caste system

Q: The man who helped India achieve independence from Great Britain through nonviolence was _____.

A: Mohandas Gandhi

Q: This major industrial and sea-port city is located on India's west coast.

A: Bombay

Q: About _____ percent of the population of India lives in cities.

A: 25

Q: Cash crops from India include _____, _____, _____, and _____.

A: tea, coffee, cashews, and tobacco

Q: Contrasts between rich and poor and between traditional and modern are especially noticeable in the city of _____.

A: Calcutta

Q: India's great river systems provide _____.

A: hydroelectric power

Q: Many people in India work in small industries that produce small consumer items such as handwoven carpets. These industries are called _____.

A: cottage industries

Q: The language used for government and business in India is _____.

A: English

Q: Most people in the northern part of India speak _____.

A: Hindi

Q: India's government is a _____.

A: democracy

Q: Most people in the southern part of India speak _____.

A: Dravidian

Q: India's first female prime minister was _____.

A: Indira Gandhi

Q: The northern river that has its source in the Himalayas and is considered holy in India is the _____ River.

A: Ganges

Q: The major religion of Pakistan is _____.

A: Islam

Q: The world's second highest mountains border Pakistan and China. Name these mountains.

A: Karakoram

Q: The most prevalent landform of southeastern Pakistan is _____.

A: desert

South Asia Bingo

		FREE		

Creative Strategies

BACKGROUND

India is a country of great diversity, yet, as with any society, people are united by shared culture traits. Although there is great diversity of people, language, and religion, India's caste system and the Hindu religion serve as two major unifying forces in Indian culture. These culture traits are most visible within the village setting. (Approximately 75% of India's population of more than 900 million people live in its more than 600,000 villages.) This activity shows students how the caste system creates an organized division of labor based on social roles. Students are divided according to the five major divisions of the caste system. The game is designed to be played with a class of 30 students; however, this may be modified depending on class size.

PROCEDURE

Give each student a copy of the handout "The Hindu Religion and Caste System of India." Have available (photocopy) the number of role cards needed. In a class of 30 students, two Brahmin, four Kshatriya, six Vaisya, eight Sudra and 10 Untouchable cards are necessary. The numbers may be adjusted depending on class size, but there must be fewer Brahmins and more Untouchables than any other caste. Fold each role card so that the information on each is hidden. To ensure fair distribution of social roles, place the role cards in a box for students to draw at random. In this way, selection of the different members of the caste system will be left to "fate."

Room arrangement

Arrange chairs in the classroom according to social caste in the following manner. Place two chairs on the front row for Brahmins, four chairs on the second row for Kshatriyas, six chairs on the third row for Vaisyas, eight chairs on the fourth row for the Sudras, and **no** chairs available for the Untouchables. Again, the number of chairs in each row should be adjusted depending on the class size.

Method

Students should NOT look at their role cards until all cards have been drawn. When students have randomly selected a "social role," they should read their cards, and follow all the instructions. Since the Untouchables are required to pick up papers around the room, you may wish to scatter a few scraps of paper

RECOMMENDED TIME

- One to two class periods

OBJECTIVES

- Understand how social organization functions as a unifying force in Indian society
- Understand the relationship between India's caste system and the Hindu religion
- Understand how social systems exist to provide society with an organized way of life

MATERIALS

- Handout: "The Hindu Religion and Caste System of India"
- Caste System Role Cards for each student
- Rewards for students as shown on role cards (teacher's choice)

on the floor before beginning the game. After sitting down in their assigned seats (Brahmins in front row, and so on) members of each social group will stand and read their cards to the rest of the class. After reading their cards, each group is given the appropriate "reward." Point out to students that these special rewards represent good or bad *karma*. While the game is in progress, you may also wish to highlight other aspects of the caste system, such as following one's *dharma* without complaint in hopes of *reincarnation* into a higher caste in one's next life. This will be especially interesting to the group of "Untouchables," who may resent their roles.

Rewards

The rewards listed on each role card should be distributed to the Brahmin, Kshatriya, Vaisyas, and Sudra members after each group has read its cards. When you (as a Brahmin) and the other members of society decide that the Untouchables have performed their social role satisfactorily, the Untouchables may then line up and be rewarded. (The reward system may be determined in any way you think is appropriate.)

Debriefing

When the game has ended, evaluate students on their understanding of the social roles in India and their relationship to the Hindu religion. Use the following questions to initiate class discussion.

1. "What did you learn about the Hindu religion or social roles in India?"

2. "How many Brahmins were there compared to Untouchables? What can you infer from this?"

3. "Why do you think this social system developed?"

4. "How does belief in *reincarnation* reinforce adherence to these social roles?"

5. "What are the major beliefs of Hinduism?"

THE HINDU RELIGION AND CASTE SYSTEM OF INDIA

HINDUISM is the religion of approximately 83 percent of the population of India. There are three major points to remember about the Hindu religion.

1. Hindus believe in *reincarnation,* which teaches that a person is born, lives, dies, and is reborn again many times.

2. Hindus believe in *karma*, which states that a person's social position in the next life depends upon his/her conduct in the present life.

3. Hindus believe in *dharma*, which provides a code of behavior or set of moral and ethical rules governing the conduct of each social class. An upper class Hindu and a lower class Hindu have different sets of rules or *dharmas* to live by.

The caste system is a type of social organization in which a person's occupation and position in life is determined by the circumstances of his/her birth. People are born into a particular caste and remain a part of that caste all of their life. Although the government of India has attempted to abolish the caste system, such long standing traditions do not easily die. The caste system, however, is less prevalent in the cities of India but remains very visible in villages. Though there are thousands of castes and subcastes, the five major divisions are:

1. priests/teachers (Brahmin)

2. warriors (Kshatriya)

3. merchants/farmers (Vaisya)

4. laborers (Sudra)

5. Untouchables (so low that they are actually *outside* the caste system and are not a caste)

CASTE SYSTEM ROLE CARDS

THIS IS YOUR SOCIAL ROLE:

1. You are Aryan.

2. You are a member of the *Brahmin Caste* and are a priest or a teacher.

3. Because you were born into this caste, you will receive the rights and privileges given all members of your group, including:
   a. 3 points on your next assignment
   b. (optional reward)

4. You must sit in a front row chair.

5. You may not marry or associate with anyone of a lower class.

THIS IS YOUR SOCIAL ROLE:

1. You are Aryan.

2. You are a member of the *Kshatriya Caste* and are a warrior.

3. Because you were born into this caste, you will receive the rights and privileges given all members of your group, including:
   a. 2 points on your next assignment
   b. (optional reward)

4. You must sit in a second row chair and be respectful to Brahmins.

5. You may not marry or associate with anyone of lower class or complain about your social role.

THIS IS YOUR SOCIAL ROLE:

1. You are Aryan.

2. You are a member of the *Vaisya Caste* and are a merchant or farmer.

3. Because you were born into this caste, you will receive the rights and privileges given all members of your group, including:
   a. 1 point on your next assignment
   b. (optional reward)

4. You must sit in a third row chair and be respectful to Brahmins and Kshatriyas.

5. You may not marry or associate with anyone of lower class or complain about your social role.

THIS IS YOUR SOCIAL ROLE:

1. You are Aryan.

2. You are a member of the *Sudra Caste* and are a skilled artisan or laborer.

3. Because you were born into this caste, you have few privileges.
   a. You do not receive extra points on your next assignment.
   b. (optional reward)
   c. If you complain, your next life will be worse than your present life.

4. You must be very respectful at all times to members of higher castes.

5. You must sit in the fourth row chair.

THIS IS YOUR SOCIAL ROLE:

1. You are Dravidian.

2. You are an *Untouchable* and must perform the dirtiest jobs in your society, such as cleaning the streets or disposing of dead bodies.

3. Because you were born an Untouchable, you have no privileges and must do everything any other caste member tells you to do.

4. In order to receive a reward, you must first clean the floor and then sit on the floor in the back of the room.

IF YOU DO NOT PERFORM YOUR DUTIES CHEERFULLY, YOUR NEXT LIFE WILL BE ONE OF UNBELIEVABLE MISERY AND YOU WILL DESERVE EVERY BAD THING THAT HAPPENS.

By the way, cows are allowed to roam the streets freely.

Building an Ecosystem: The Great Barrier Reef

Creative Strategies

BACKGROUND

The Great Barrier Reef, which lies from 20 to 100 miles off the coast of Queensland, Australia, stretches more than 1,250 miles long and varies in width from 10 to 100 miles. It is one of nature's most complex ecosystems. Tiny coral are the architects of the reef and are present in an incredible variety of shapes, colors, and sizes—from fragile fan-shaped coral to huge lumps of brain coral perhaps six- feet thick and weighing up to several tons. Development of the reef occurs in three phases: from polyp to colony to reef. The colonies all begin with a single coral polyp which secretes its stony substance in numerous varieties of shapes and patterns. The most prevalent type on the Great Barrier Reef is staghorn-shaped coral. The Great Barrier Reef contains thousands of colonies made up of billions of coral polyps, which are bound together by limestone-secreting algae. The exact number of varieties of plants and animals within the Great Barrier Reef system is unknown. The myriad creatures of the reef survive by developing mutually beneficial relationships. While the reef is a highly competitive habitat, it is nevertheless a successful biome, balanced by these interdependent relationships. Some of the relationships of the Great Barrier Reef system are given in the script, "Building an Ecosystem."

PROCEDURE

Organize students into small groups and give each student a copy of the script. Students will gain insight into the nature of ecosystems through role play. Each group will assume the role of one of the "building blocks" of the coral reef ecosystem. Students should be familiar with the terms ecosystem, biome, and habitat.

There are 12 roles. If the role play is conducted with a class of 30 students, one student should be selected as Narrator, three students represent the Waters of the South Pacific Ocean, three students are Coral Polyps, three are Algae, two are Blue Wrasses, three represent anemones, three are Clown Fish, three are Parrot Fish, three are other Tropical Fish, two are Crown of Thorns Starfish, two are Triton Clams and two students represent people. These numbers should be modified according to class size. It is important that all students be involved in the reading.

RECOMMENDED TIME

- One-half to one class period

OBJECTIVES

- Recognize the inter-dependence of life systems of a coral reef

MATERIALS

- Handout: (Script) "Building An Ecosystem: The Great Barrier Reef" for each student
- Encyclopedias or other reference materials

After the class has read the script, debriefing should occur. Call on volunteers to answer the following questions.

What facts about ecosystems were illustrated?

What were some of the relationships found in this ecosystem?

How is this ecosystem like all other ecosystems?

What would happen if a part of the ecosystem were removed?

What would happen if the waters became polluted?

Extending the Activity

Have students create collages or drawings of the reef biome illustrating interdependent relationships of the ecosystem at work. Suggest that students show the impact of people on the biome as well. In addition, suggest that interested students work together to research other biomes in Australia or in the world, such as rain forests, or deserts, and then create a script similar to "'Building an Ecosystem." They might create visuals, such as flow charts, collages, or illustrations that stress the interdependent relationships within each biome.

REFERENCES

Lawler, Clarrie. *The Great Barrier Reef.* Sydney: Australian Universities Press Pty. Ltd., 1974.

Melham, Tom. "The Coral Reefs," *The Ocean Realm.* Washington, D.C.: The National Geographic Society, 1978.

Cousteau, Jacques. *The Ocean World.* New York: Abradale Press/Harry N. Abrams, Inc., 1985.

BUILDING AN ECOSYSTEM: THE GREAT BARRIER REEF

NARRATOR:
An ecosystem is the relationship among all living and non-living things in a particular environment. There are thousands of relationships in the great barrier reef ecosystem. These relationships, however, must remain in balance or the system will be destroyed.

WATERS OF THE SOUTH PACIFIC OCEAN:
We are the warm, clear waters of the south Pacific ocean near the continent of Australia. Because our water temperature never drops below 68 degrees, we can support many kinds of sea life. We are the home of Australia's great barrier reef, which is more than 1,200 miles long.

CORAL POLYPS:
We are tiny little coral polyps that live only in warm tropical waters. We look like colorful plants but we are really tiny animals and are only about a tenth of an inch in size. We may be tiny, but we are the architects of the entire reef biome.

We live on top of the limestone skeletons of dead polyps. Because we are so tiny, it takes four years for the reef to grow one-fourth of an inch. Can you understand why it took millions of years for the great barrier reef to form?

ALGAE:
We are algae, the tiny plants that grow with the coral on the great barrier reef. We grow so well in these waters that thousands of little fish swim by and have us for a tasty meal.

We are simple plants, but don't think we aren't important. We can do amazing things like change carbon dioxide, water, and sunlight into food and provide coral with oxygen and the nutrients they need to construct the rock walls on which they live. But, of course we also get something in return for helping the coral. The coral walls provide us with a protected habitat. Coral also gives us the carbon dioxide we need for photosynthesis.

WATERS OF THE SOUTH PACIFIC OCEAN:
The relationship between the coral and algae is just one example from the thousands of interrelationships within the coral reef habitat. You can see that if our water becomes polluted and dirty, the sunlight will be blocked and their special relationship will be destroyed.

BLUE CLEANER WRASSE FISH:
We are just one small part of the biome of the reef but we are very important to reef ecology. Without us, many other fish would become unhealthy and perhaps even die. Our special cleaning stations in caves or overhangs built by the coral are visited by all sizes of fish. Even huge manta rays open their mouths and spread their fins for a thorough cleaning. We are very special fish because we clean the other fish by eating the parasites which infest their bodies.

SEA ANEMONES:
Most people think we are plants, but we are relatives of coral. We love these warm, clear south Pacific waters. All day, our hundreds of tentacles wave with the ocean currents and food on the reef is abundant.

CLOWN FISH:
The anemones speak as if they had no helpers to produce their abundant supply of food. If it wasn't for us, they would not be so well fed and probably would not survive for very long in this complex environment. After all, we are one of the most colorful fish in these waters. Our beauty attracts larger fish as we swim in and out of the protective tentacles of our anemone hosts. We are very specialized little clowns.

SEA ANEMONES:
The clowns are very specialized little fish all right! They are immune to our poisonous tentacles, but the larger fish they attract are not. Once in the grasp of our stinging tentacles, the larger fish are goners! But we are not greedy, we share our delicious meal with our little clown fish partners.

PARROT FISH:
Can you guess why we are called parrot fish? It's not because we are such large fish. Yes, it has to do with our beautiful colors. We

always have the munchies and we munch on coral rock, giving it back as the white sands of our ocean floor. Some of us even eat the coral that build our special environment. Sounds like we could be very destructive, doesn't it? But alas, big-toothed barracudas have the munchies too. **For us!** So you can see, it all balances out and our ecosystem stays healthy.

OTHER TROPICAL FISH:
We are the many other beautiful tropical fish that swim in the warm south Pacific waters. There are so many of us that it is hard to believe that we all have our own special role to play in the coral reef ecosystem.

We love the tasty algae that grow on the coral skeletons. But we are fish, not pigs, and we do not destroy the algae by eating too much. Some of us even have pointy mouths so that we do not damage the delicate coral when we eat. Can you understand how we all depend on each other for survival in our ecosystem?

Oh, no! Here come the crown of thorns starfish. They eat like pigs and will destroy the coral reef if something isn't done!

NARRATOR:
The coral, algae, and fish form some of the relationships on the barrier reef. The live coral live on the skeletons of the dead coral. The structure provides a home for the algae. The little fish eat the algae. This part of the ecosystem is in balance. But if there are too many crown of thorns starfish they will destroy the natural balance of the ecosystem.

CROWN OF THORNS STARFISH:
We are the crown of thorns starfish and we multiply very rapidly when coral reefs are not protected by our natural enemy, the triton clams. Unfortunately, we are not too bright and don't know that when we eat all the coral, the reef will die and so will we.

NARRATOR:
The presence of too many starfish in the ecosystem is about to cause a disaster to the reef. This is an example of what happens when there is a change in the harmonious relationships that are shared by the creatures of the reef.

TRITON CLAMS:
Don't worry coral, algae, and little fish. We have colorful shells to attract the starfish. We will catch and eat enough starfish for dinner to keep our reef system in balance. As long as we are a part of this ecosystem, we will control the size of the starfish population.

PEOPLE:
We are the tourists who love the coral reef. In fact, we just love it **to death**. At low tide we like to walk on the reef and collect large pieces of coral to take home and show our friends.

NARRATOR:
I wonder if these people know how many years of growth they are destroying. For every inch of coral they take home they are destroying 16 years of growth. If 100 people each take only one inch of coral, sixteen hundred years of growth on the barrier reef is gone.

PEOPLE:
This coral reef is so beautiful, especially those giant pink triton clam shells. These will make great souvenirs.

NARRATOR:
But the next time the people came to the reef it was dead. The people had destroyed the builders of the reef, the coral polyps. They had taken the triton clam shells, the natural enemy of the crown of thorns starfish, and had upset the entire ecosystem.

PEOPLE:
The reef is ugly and the waters are all polluted. All the beautiful tropical fish are gone. What happened?

ALL THE CREATURES OF THE REEF:
We are all perfectly adapted to our own special environments within the reef. But we are all interrelated. Even the slightest change in our environment can cause a chain reaction, killing us all.

NARRATOR:
An ecosystem is the relationship among all living and non-living things in a particular environment. When these relationships are destroyed, the ecosystem dies.

Creative Strategies

BACKGROUND

Settled by Great Britain in 1788 as a prison colony, Australia today is a modern and prosperous democratic nation. It is the sixth largest country in the world, with a land area about the same size as the contigous United States. Because it lies south of the equator, Australia is sometimes called the "Land Down Under."

The nation is made up of six states and two federal territories. The states include New South Wales, Victoria, Queensland, South Australia, Western Australia, and the island state of Tasmania. The two federal territories are the Northern Territory and the tiny Australian Capital Territory, in which Canberra, the national capital, is located. Australia also governs several small islands in the South Pacific and Indian oceans. The Australian population is concentrated in a few large coastal cities. The rest of the continent, known as the Outback, is dry, flat, ad almost uninhabited.

PROCEDURE

Give each student a copy of the Australian slang words and an instruction sheet. Explain that they are to write an original story about an imaginary trip to Australia, incorporating Australian slang words. This activity reinforces concepts and facts about Australia. The instructions given in this lesson plan can be modified to stress information that you believe is most important. The lesson may be used as a cooperative learning activity when students work in pairs or in groups of no more than three. Working with a partner often eases the insecurity some students have about creating their own work. In addition, students generally learn from each other in the process of working together.

Call on volunteers to read their stories aloud to the rest of the class. Grading should be based on the amount of factual information given about Australia and how well the slang words are incorporated into the story.

REFERENCE

Story idea from Alice M. Davis, Stephen F. Austin High School, Austin, Texas.

RECOMMENDED TIME
- One class period

OBJECTIVE
- Develop creative writing skills

MATERIALS
- Handout: "Instructions: Australian Slang" for each student
- Handout: "Australian Slang Words" for each student

INSTRUCTIONS: AUSTRALIAN SLANG

Use the list of Australian slang words, and your vivid imagination to write an original story three to four pages long describing your recent visit to Australia.

Use as many Australian slang words as possible in your story and underline each one. Be creative and make this assignment interesting and fun!

Grading will be based on the amount of factual information given about Australia and how well slang words are incorporated into this information.

AUSTRALIAN SLANG WORDS

Pushy: bicycle

True Blue Aussie: genuine Australian

Fair Dinkum!: "For real," as in "No joke" or "You're not kidding"

Yobbo: a person who acts thoughtlessly without thinking

Shanghai: slingshot

Bum: person's behind

Fag: cigarette

Sunnies: sunglasses

Bawling: crying

Good on Ya!: good job, nice going

Wino: bum

Dunny: restroom with just a toilet

Dagbag: backpack for school books, etc.

Biscuit: cookie

G'day: "Hello" or "What's up?"

G'day mate: greeting a boy or man

G'day love: greeting a girl or woman

Scone: biscuit or roll

Bushie: a person who lives in the outback

Bikie: a person who rides a motorcycle, is large. wears sunnies, and travels around with other motorcycle riders.

Truckie: truck driver

Petrol: gasoline

Boot: car trunk

Bonnet: hood of a car

Bloke: man

Sheila: girl or woman

Mate: friend or pal

Tucker: food

Tuck Shop: school cafeteria

Lollies: candy

Pommy: an English person

Yankie: Australian name for all Americans

Footie: Australian football rules

Walkie: journey or just a short walk

Hard Yakka: really hard work

Lemonade: 7-Up

Clicks: kilometers per hour or miles per hour

Milk Bar: soda fountain

Flat Out or Flat to the Boards: working very, very hard

Fortnight: two weeks

Torch: flashlight

Pub: bar

Mum: Mother

To Skull a Bottle: drink up without stopping

Chemist Shop: drug store

Postie: mail carrier

Cocky: cockroach

Tinny: beer

Smoko: break, as in a little time off

Strine: speaking the Australian way

Galah: politician, also a type of parrot

Cuppa: cup of tea

Blowies: blowflies

Mozzies: mosquitoes

Roo: kangaroo

Roo Bar: heavy metal guard on the front of a vehicle

Kero: kerosene

Surfie: surfboard rider

Oz: Australia

Give a Shout: buy a round of drinks

Give a Yankie Shout: everybody buys their own drink

Judder Bars: speed bumps

Banana Bender: someone who lives in Queensland

Flash Sheila: a good-looking girl

A-1 Flash Sheila: a very good-looking girl

Technicolor Yawn: to throw up

Spotties: bright spotlights on a pickup truck

Bloody Oath!: "No kidding!"

Basic Vocabulary Words and Elements of the ABCs of Culture

cultural geography/anthropology: study of *living* cultures

archaeology: study of *past* cultures

gregarious: likes to be with other people (we naturally want to be in groups that are similar to us)

cultural diffusion: borrowing from other cultures—food, clothing styles, etc.; spread of culture to another area

acculturation: process by which a person from one culture adopts traits of another culture

prejudice: unreasonable attitude or bias against a group or culture based on supposed characteristics

bias: personal, distorted judgment that influences objective perception; one-sided

stereotype: over-simplified, commonly held opinion of a person or group; often a composite of traits; generalizations about an entire group

ethnocentric: (ethno=cultural group; centric=at the center) person that believes his/her culture is the best or better than others; bad if extreme; good if establishes self-pride

xenophobia: (xeno=foreign; phobia=fear) a fear of foreigners or things foreign

"The ABCs of Culture"

Appearance: clothing (special occasions, colors, how it is worn, hats, uniforms); jewelry (special meaning—wedding ring, lapel pins); type of material (bought, handmade, imported); hair style (females in Peru: two pigtails=married; many pigtails=single); physical features (tall, short); makeup; tattoos; etc.

Belief System: religion; superstitions (all cultures have them: Last Supper—13 people there and last was Judas; salt spilled in front of him; step on a crack; lights on cars in funeral procession, etc.)

Communication: language; tone; signs; body language (82% of teacher messages are non-verbal); titles (presidents *vs* king *vs* chief); greetings (hand shakes); common words with different definitions: "Do you **mind** waiting for me?"; last names from jobs (Miller, Smith), physical features (Rivers, Hill); *Mc, von,* and *O'* all mean "son of," as in McDonald, von Huesen, O'Neill, and also Johnson, Jackson, etc.

Dates: history; ancestry; heritage; establish concepts of time—how is it important to society?; holidays; etc.

Entertainment: art; music; crafts; dance; sports; songs; storytelling; hobbies; etc.

Food: types; spices; special occasions: preparation; taboos; how people eat; number of meals a day and times eaten; fasting; etc.

Government: laws; values; titles; social roles and order (Do only women raise children? Are certain jobs reserved for men?); how people act towards each other (consider different age groups); social groups/clubs, etc.

Housing: style; materials; use of rooms; shape; size; color; arrangement of furniture; etc.

Information: informal (education from relatives and peers); formal (school, life experience)

Jobs: technology (scientific knowledge and tools); economy; ways of making a living; style/type of currency; transportation; communication; etc.

Kind of Environment: location; climate; physical features; vegetation (This information explains relationships to the environment, such as why the Inuit of the northern Arctic region eat raw meat and fish—there is no wood to burn for cooking; this also explains why there are many words in their language describing snow and ice.)

Leftovers: leftover information that doesn't fit into one of the above categories (population, diseases, etc.)

Remember that many items will fit into more than one category. Practice classifying items according to the ABCs of Culture. Determine the appropriate categories for these items: magnifying glass (J), birthday party (D), money (J).

The Mbuti of the Rain Forest

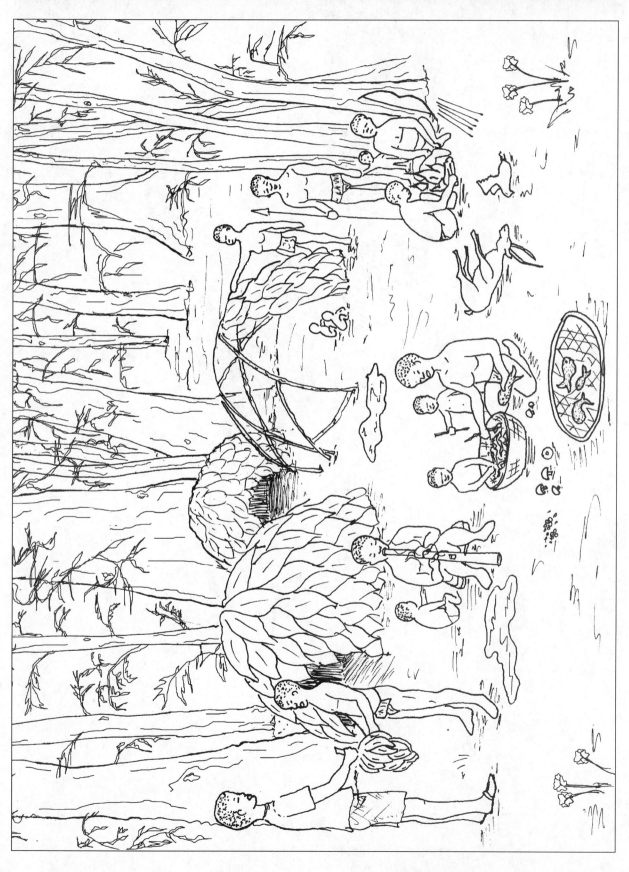

Country Description

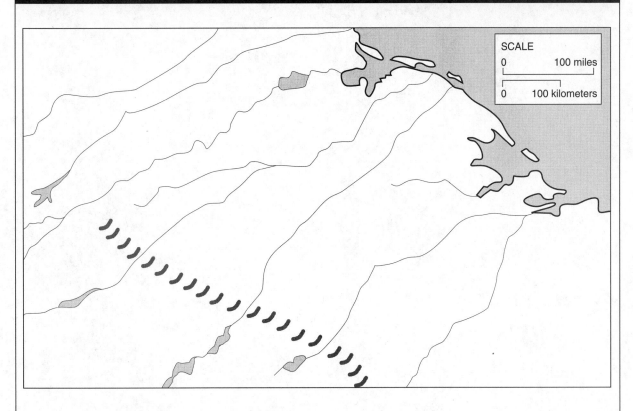

SCALE

0 _____ 100 miles

0 _____ 100 kilometers

1. Name of country _____

2. Population of country _____

3. Three largest cities and their populations _____

_____

_____

4. Capital city and its population _____

5. What do you think is the actual location of this area? _____

Map Key

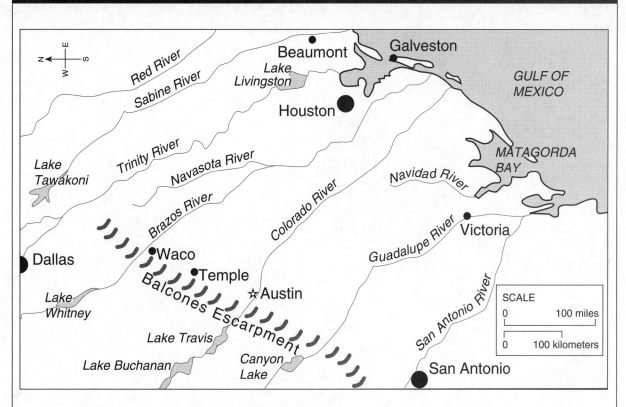

1. Name of country   <u>USA/Texas</u>

2. Population of country   <u>260,713,585 (1994)/18,031,484 (1993)</u>

3. Three largest cities and their populations (1990 census)

Houston	1,629,902
Dallas	1,007,618
San Antonio	935,393
Austin	465,648

4. Capital City

5. What do you think is the actual location of this area?   <u>South Central United States</u>

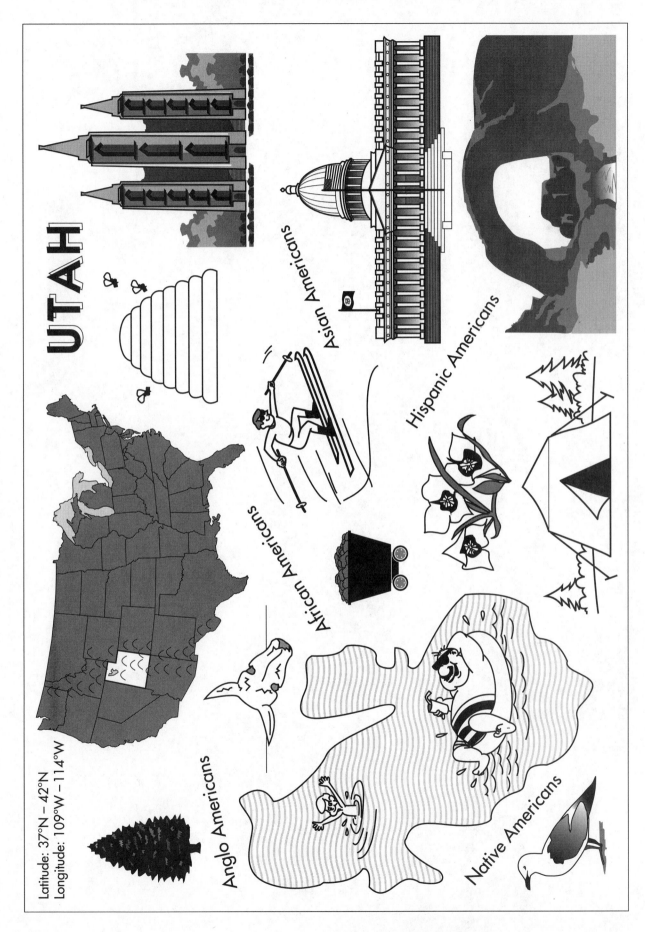

Latitude: 37°N – 42°N
Longitude: 109°W – 114°W

UTAH

Asian Americans

Hispanic Americans

African Americans

Anglo Americans

Native Americans

"Scrambled Notes" Outline Guide

I. WHAT IS THE APPROXIMATE SIZE OF RUSSIA?
   A. Russia is . . .
   B. Russia spreads . . .
   C. Russia covers . . .

II. WHAT IS THE TOPOGRAPHY OF RUSSIA LIKE?
   A. Landforms . . .
   B. Russia has . . .
   C. The rivers . . .

III. WHAT ARE THE MAIN FACTORS THAT AFFECT CLIMATE IN RUSSIA?
   A. Latitude . . .
   B. Russia covers a . . .
   C. There are . . .
   D. There is . . .

IV. WHAT ARE RUSSIA'S TEMPERATURES LIKE?
   A. Temperatures . . .
   B. Winters . . .

V. HOW ARE THE PEOPLE OF RUSSIA AFFECTED BY THE CLIMATE?
   A. Life . . .
   B. Many . . .
   C. *Permafrost* . . .

VI. WHAT IS THE RELATIONSHIP BETWEEN VEGETATION AND CLIMATE IN RUSSIA?
   A. The most . . .
   B. The . . .
   C. The . . .
   D. Most . . .

VII. WHAT KINDS OF NATURAL RESOURCES ARE FOUND IN RUSSIA?
   A. Russia has . . .
   B. The Central . . .

"Scrambled Notes" Outline Key

I. WHAT IS THE APPROXIMATE SIZE OF RUSSIA?
  A. Russia is larger than the U.S. and Mexico combined.
  B. Russia spreads over two continents, Europe and Asia.
  C. Russia covers 6,000 miles from west to east and has 11 time zones.

II. WHAT IS THE TOPOGRAPHY OF RUSSIA LIKE?
  A. Landforms consist mainly of plains, but there are some mountains. The large number of plains affect the climate because there are no mountain ranges to block the cold winds that blow across Russia from the Arctic.
  B. Russia has a large coastline, but it is frozen most of the year. This affects the economy because it is difficult to import and export goods.
  C. The rivers of Russia are important because they provide hydroelectric power, transportation, trade, and access to the seas. However, many rivers flow north and are frozen part of the year.

III. WHAT ARE THE MAIN FACTORS THAT AFFECT CLIMATE IN RUSSIA?
  A. Latitude affects climate because much of Russia is located in the higher (colder) latitudes.
  B. Russia covers a huge land area and has a continental climate. Because there are many areas that do not receive the moderating effects of large bodies of water, the climate has great extremes of temperature, from very hot to very cold.
  C. There are few mountain barriers in the north to block cold arctic winds, but the Himalayas block the warm moist air from the south.
  D. There is a large spread in latitude, which also affects the range of climate.

IV. WHAT ARE RUSSIA'S TEMPERATURES LIKE?
  A. Temperatures of 30 to 40 degrees below zero are not uncommon, and it is even colder in Siberia.
  B. Winters are long and cold and the summers are short and often hot. There is little spring or fall.

V. HOW ARE THE PEOPLE OF RUSSIA AFFECTED BY THE CLIMATE?
  A. Life is difficult because the climate is so harsh. Travel is difficult, and there are very few ports that are free of ice during the long winters.
  B. Many citizens vacation in the warmest area they can find. The warmest area is located near the Black Sea where there is a Mediterranean climate.
  C. *Permafrost* in the higher (colder) regions of Russia causes many problems. People must build their houses in special ways to prevent tilting and cracking of the foundations during the summer thawing of the frozen soil.

VI. WHAT IS THE RELATIONSHIP BETWEEN VEGETATION AND CLIMATE IN RUSSIA?
  A. The most northern part of Russia has a polar climate. The vegetation in this zone is *tundra*.
  B. The subpolar climate vegetation is *taiga,* which means "needleleaf forest."
  C. The steppes of Russia have a dry climate, and the vegetation here is short grasses and scattered trees.
  D. Most areas of Russia are too dry or too cold for growing crops. Most crops are grown in the steppe regions.

VII. WHAT KINDS OF NATURAL RESOURCES ARE FOUND IN RUSSIA?
  A. Russia has an abundance of natural resources, such as forests, oil and natural gas, coal, metals, and diamonds.
  B. The Central Siberian Plateau, located between the Yenisei and Lena rivers, has many minerals which have not been tapped.

Climographs

STATION _Almaty, Kazakhstan_ **CLIMATIC TYPE** _highland_
LAT. _43° 16'_ **LONG.** _76° 53'_ **MEAN ANNUAL TEMP.** _44.5°_
MEAN ANNUAL RANGE OF TEMP. _56°_
ANNUAL PRECIP. _23.5"_   **ELEV.** _2543'_

STATION _____ **CLIMATIC TYPE** _____
LAT. _____ **LONG.** _____ **MEAN ANNUAL TEMP.** _____
MEAN ANNUAL RANGE OF TEMP. _____
ANNUAL PRECIP. _____   **ELEV.** _____

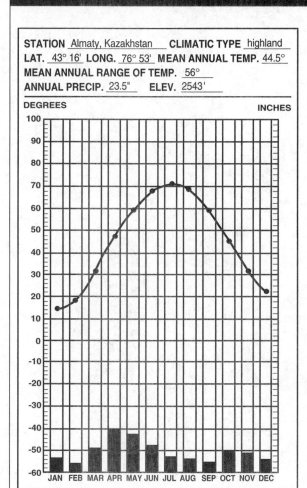

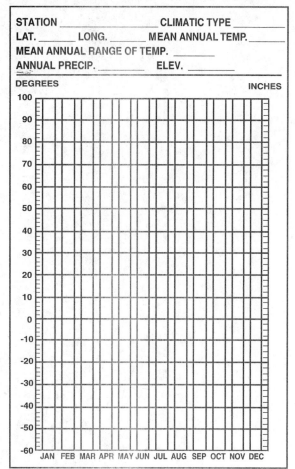

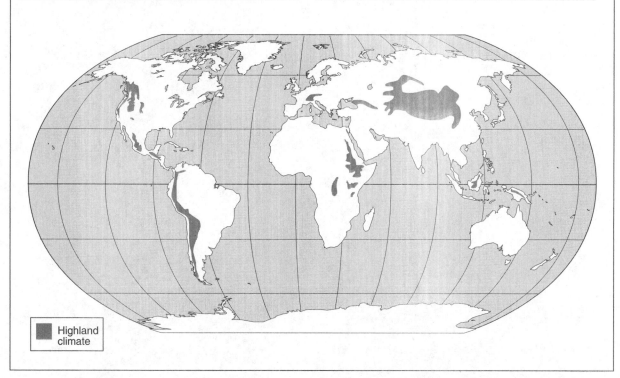

Highland climate

Ways to Wear a *Kanga*

Skirt

Adapted from *Kangas: 101 Uses* by Jeannette Hanby with drawings by David Bygott. Copyright © 1984 by Jeannette Hanby and David Bygott. Reprinted by permission of *Jeannette Hanby and David Bygott*.

Shawl

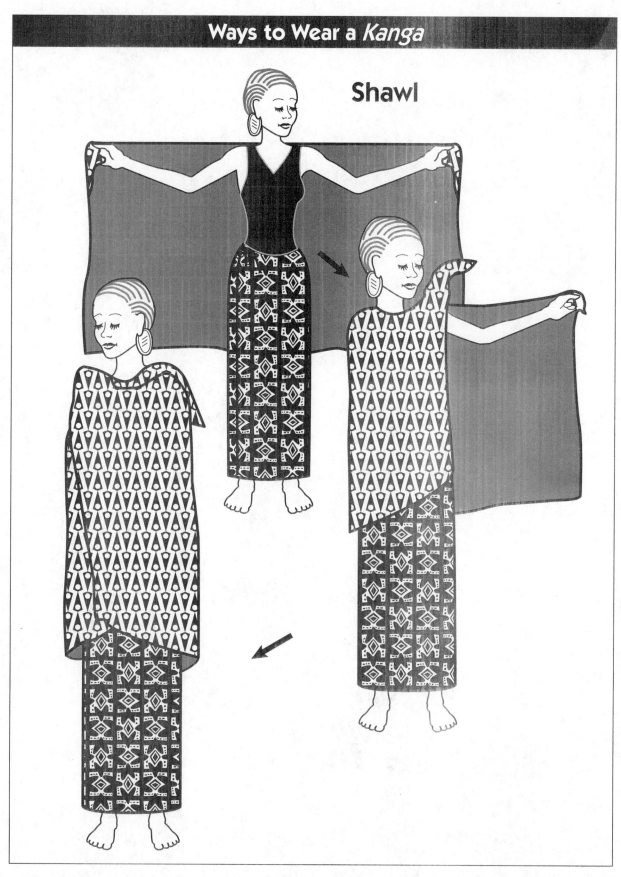

Adapted from *Kangas: 101 Uses* by Jeannette Hanby with drawings by David Bygott. Copyright © 1984 by Jeannette Hanby and David Bygott. Reprinted by permission of *Jeannette Hanby and David Bygott*.

Ways to Wear a *Kanga*

Dress

Chest knot

Behind-neck knot

Adapted from *Kangas: 101 Uses* by Jeannette Hanby with drawings by David Bygott. Copyright © 1984 by Jeannette Hanby and David Bygott. Reprinted by permission of *Jeannette Hanby and David Bygott.*

Ways to Wear a Kanga

Headpiece

Fold diagonally and roll into narrow strip.

Place at back of head.

Tuck in loose ends and wrap firmly around head.

Knot over forehead.

Swimsuit

Adapted from *Kangas: 101 Uses* by Jeannette Hanby with drawings by David Bygott. Copyright © 1984 by Jeannette Hanby and David Bygott. Reprinted by permission of *Jeannette Hanby and David Bygott.*

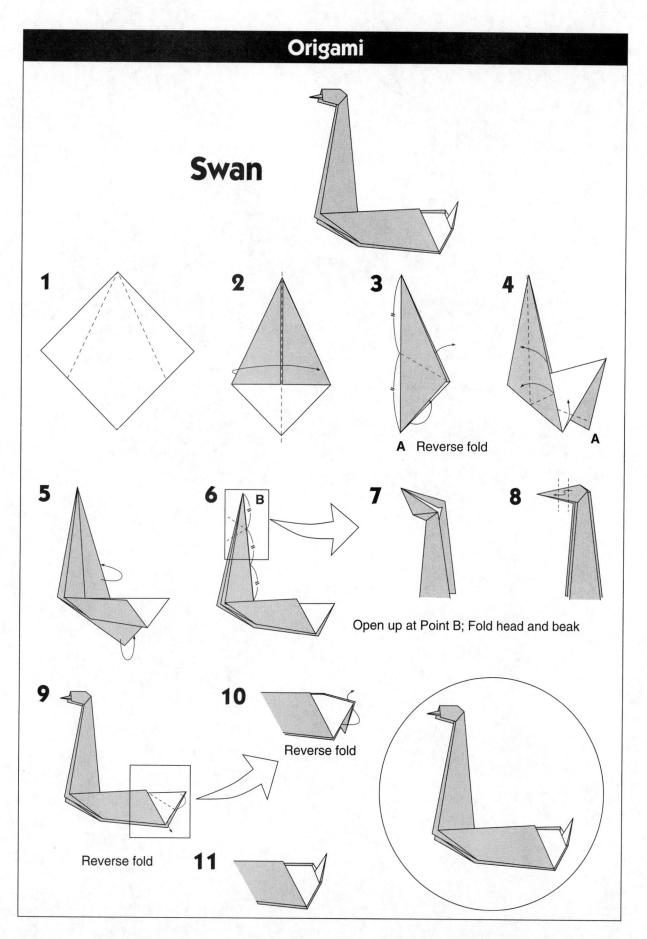

Swan

1

2

3

A Reverse fold

4

A

5

6 B

Open up at Point B; Fold head and beak

7

8

9

10

Reverse fold

Reverse fold

11

South Asia Bingo

		FREE		